TRUE VISION 4 SUCCESS

BOB NATOLI

True Vision 4

SUCCESS

Bob Natoli Achievement Systems
New York

Published by Bob Natoli Achievement Systems
113-119 East Bridge Street
Oswego, NY 13126

First edition. First printing.
Printed in the United States of America.
Design and composition by BW&A Books, Inc.

ISBN: 978-0-9828769-0-9

This book is designed to provide information in regard to self-improvement.
However, its primary objective is to entertain and inform. The author and all
who had a hand in creating this work assume no liability and no responsibility to any person or entity with respect to any loss, damage caused or alleged
to be caused, directly or indirectly, by the information in this book. Also,
before embarking on any exercise program or change of diet and lifestyle,
always seek advice from your doctor.

For this reason a man will leave his father and mother
and be united to his wife, and they will become one flesh.

It is to my wife Peggy who has been so much a part of me
that I want to dedicate this book. You alone, sweetheart,
saw something in me that you chose to believe in so many
years ago. Because of the love and faith that you continue
to have in me I will continue to move forward in success.
Know that my love will always be with you and that
whatever I have been fortunate enough to accomplish
was always done with you in my heart and mind.

CONTENTS

LUNCH WITH A MILLIONAIRE

Have you ever wondered what it might be like to sit down with a millionaire for lunch and ask him the reasons for his success—about how he made his millions? What were his secrets? Exactly how did he do it?—AND could he please tell you how you could do it too?

I have had lunch with the millionaire who wrote this book. As a matter of fact, I've worked with Bob Natoli for many years. My company, Anthony Wellman Productions, has produced numerous radio commercials for his different ventures over the past two decades, so I've come to know this entrepreneurial powerhouse named Bob Natoli pretty well. And let me tell you, you would be hard-pressed to find anyone more thoroughly dedicated to self-improvement and personal success than Bob.

This incredibly enthusiastic guy is always looking for ways to improve himself, his businesses or whatever project he sets his mind to. From the day I met him I quickly discovered he was constantly on the lookout for knowledge, zestfully seeking ideas and opportunities to improve his health, his business, and his overall life. He always seemed to have his nose in some book that could teach him something new. Even time on the road was spent learning. In his car you would typically find one or more how-to audiotapes and a pile of books sitting in the backseat. When he wasn't reading or running his businesses he was improving himself physically at the gym or learning about food and nutrition.

As a result of his concentrated efforts over these past twenty-five years Bob has created significant wealth for himself, his family and his community. Not to mention the thousands of people for whom he's provided jobs.

Bob didn't inherit millions, though he did inherit good values from his family and lessons from his mother and father. Otherwise, he began with nothing but his own dreams and found ways to turn those dreams into a reality. He started a company called Rentavision from scratch with a single store and proceeded to expand that to a booming 250 stores covering 16 states and employing over 1,000 people. His achievements were formally recognized when he won the regional Ernst & Young Entrepreneur of the Year Award sponsored by *USA Today*, NASDAQ, and the Kauffman Center For Entrepreneurial Leadership. Eventually he sold Rentavision for close to $100 million. Today he is a successful real estate investor while simultaneously launching yet another chain of stores. He's not up to 250 of them yet but he has several up and running now with highly focused plans for more. Bob is nothing if not goal-oriented and persistent.

Yes, Bob has found what many people would define as success when measured by bank accounts. However, he is successful in other ways as well. He and his wife have forged a solid marriage. While the national divorce rate hovers around 50%, he and Peggy have been happily married for 25 years, and along the way have even helped other couples through marriage counseling. They have two healthy children who are now finding their own pathways to success.

He has also found success as an athlete and has been recognized by GUINNESS WORLD RECORDS three times: two for the most chin-ups in one minute and one for the most squat thrusts in one minute. Bob considers good health a very critical measure of success because it's harder (not impossible, just more challenging) to achieve any other kind of success without good health to begin with.

Yet for all his triumphs Bob would be the first to tell you he's not perfect, just a human being, the same as you or I. He doesn't claim to be a genius or unusually gifted. But he has worked very hard at learning what this thing called "success" really is—and how to reach out and help himself to a share of it.

Money, of course, is only one measure of success. There are others. Maybe you're not interested so much in making millions of dollars as you are in finding some other kind of success.

This is a book about making your dreams come true, whatever they may be: fame, wealth, health, a happy family life—anywhere your dreams may take you. People may define success in different ways but most will probably agree that making your dreams come true is certainly one of them.

For getting to the how-tos of success from the source himself, reading this book is as good as sitting down to lunch with millionaire Bob Natoli. Actually it's better because within these pages you will find a lot more information than could ever be covered during the course of a single lunch. Bob has taken the time to set it all down, a step by step roadmap for achievement.

Bob Natoli found success by identifying and pursuing his goals with the very same True Vision strategies you will find within these pages. He is now offering you a chance to do the same.

Anthony Wellman
Fairfield, Connecticut
August 2010

chapter one

WHAT IS THAT DRIVING FORCE?

A vision is not just a picture of what could be;
it is an appeal to our better selves,
a call to become something more.
  —Rosabeth Moss Kanter

What is that driving force that sweeps one person to success yet never touches the life of another? I have not only lived my own success story but have helped others achieve success as well. By learning to harness this very force I have had the opportunity to put into action exciting and successful techniques, changing lives for the better. I have watched people soar to the top of their chosen fields or achieve their heart's desire by using this methodology.

This certain something seems to lie dormant in most people but is obvious in those who have achieved success in any particular area of their life. This driving force is within the person who loses fifty pounds, and within the person who suddenly gives up a lifelong smoking habit. It is there in abundance with those who have the drive to start a business. In fact, it exists to some degree in *every* successful undertaking, great or small!

You may be happy to learn that this driving force which you, too, can harness and which will help lead you to success in whatever your quest may be, has nothing to do with how tall or attractive you are. It has nothing to do with how much money you may currently have. Nor does it have anything to do with your educational level, your upbringing, or even the person to whom you are married. This certain something that must be present for you to be able to climb your personal mountain is already within you as you read these words. It currently lies just beneath the surface, like an underground geyser waiting to be tapped. When you learn the methodologies in this book, this force will spring forward with all of the personal motivation and skills that are needed to accomplish exactly what you want in life.

This essential resource that is found in every success story is called True Vision. The stronger your True Vision, the less chance there is for failure; but without it, you cannot succeed for very long. True Vision is the driving force that is able to change lives for the better. This book is about succeeding. The first and most important element in every success is possession, and cultivation, of your True Vision. Your own personal Vision might be to lose fifty pounds, to stop smoking, to make a fortune or to just get out of debt. Your success depends upon your True Vision, and nothing else. Deep inside all of us is a True Vision for how we want our lives to be, and it is my sincerest wish that after reading this book you will be able to harness your own True Vision.

I believe that each of us is born with certain skills and abilities that we are meant to utilize. While we learn from struggle and failure, when we possess True Vision our ultimate destiny will be success, however we define it. A life that has True Vision is one that is developed to its full capacity. You can be sure that when you learn the importance of having True Vision, and utilize the successful techniques included in this book, you will be well on your way to achieving the success you have always wanted in whatever endeavor your True Vision path takes you.

What Is True Vision?

What do I mean when I say the words True Vision? My definition of True Vision is establishing a genuine, unquestionable, positive, vivid picture in your mind's eye of exactly what you want to do, one that will satisfy you and give you a more fulfilling life. It is based upon your own desires, talents and what you are capable of learning. Since you are a unique individual with your own particular desires, your True Vision, like DNA, is most likely going to be at least a little different than someone else's, just as you look and act a bit differently than everyone else. And together you and I are going to discover and cultivate a True

Vision for you within your mind's eye, and help you develop a skill-set to get you there.

How many people wake up each morning and purposely look for ways to make themselves unhappy? Yet, that is exactly what some do. This is partly because they have no True Vision for their life, and may end up in a job they are not particularly happy with. Sometimes their problem is more personal; they never look or feel quite the way they want. It could be that their relationships with family members, friends, or even coworkers are flat and unsatisfying. When you don't have a vision of where you are going you tend to wind up in a place you don't really want to be. Fortunately, it's never too late to reverse the things that keep us stuck and stalemated. We can do this when we create our own True Vision.

There may be something missing in your life, something you want to accomplish, or something that you have been struggling with and have not yet found a way to defeat. The purpose of this book is to assist you in obtaining what you really want out of your life, and, for those of you who are uncertain, even to help you figure out what that is. Life, as we know, moves forward, sometimes presenting us with challenges that dictate that we make new beginnings. Some challenges seem to find us, in the form of a habit that seemingly cannot be broken, a defeatist attitude that holds us back, or a sudden change in our financial condition that is thrust upon us without much warning. Other times it is we who willingly decide to go forth to climb new mountains or set sail on strange and distant waters. Finding successful methods for dealing with these challenges and for creating opportunities for making positive changes is what this book is all about. Finding your True Vision is the beginning of victory in dealing with life's challenges.

This book is the culmination of all my personal, hands-on experience, along with other successful strategies which I believe will help you succeed. I have taken my own True Vision into the real world and succeeded. In a sense you are fortunate because by reading this book you will be able to avoid mistakes that I've made along the way. I've very carefully separated what works from methods that look like they should work, but never bear positive results. This book will show you how to capture your True Vision and then, step-by-step, point you in the direction that you need to go in order to make it a reality.

I have not succeeded in life because I am necessarily smarter, better educated or even better looking than other people (although my wife thinks I am all of these). The only reason that I've succeeded is that I have learned, understood, and obeyed the one true success formula that everyone uses who has succeeded (even if they don't know they're using it). Some who have found success may not have given credit to their True Vision, or even been aware they've employed it; nonetheless they have all succeeded because of this method.

Regardless of what you may have heard, it is not luck that determines success. You don't see many people who are walking around forty pounds lighter, smoke free, or wealthy because of luck. No, luck actually has little to do with it. Rather, the rules of success determine for the most part whether you succeed or fail, nothing more. The rules of lasting success start with obtaining True Vision. It was Lee Trevino, the professional golfer, from whom I first heard these words: "The more I practice the luckier I get." A Mexican American who fought his way out of poverty to become one of golf's most notable players, Trevino well understood that luck is not a pathway to success.

No, luck is not the answer. Like any other endeavor success has its own rules. If you don't know these rules but accidentally break them you'll be wondering why you've not yet succeeded. Like the law of gravity, you may not know it exists, but if you jump from the top of a building you'll soon see the immediate power that it has over you. These rules of success apply to you no matter what the goal is that you are trying to achieve. Whether it's losing weight or starting your own business, you need to understand that the steps to success are virtually the same. That's one reason why you often see those who have been successful at one endeavor also achieve success in other areas of their life. Still others seem to work hard but never really get anywhere. Maybe I've just described someone you know.

The very qualities that go into making someone a success in one area of their life are the same qualities that can assist them in whatever they are trying to accomplish. One example of a person with True Vision is Arnold Schwarzenegger.

Arnold Schwarzenegger, Immigrant, Bodybuilder, Movie Star & Governor

He was only six years old living in a small Austrian town when his father took him to a nearby city to see former Olympic gold medalist and movie star Johnny Weissmuller dedicate a new swimming pool. As soon as little Arnold set his eyes on this Olympic champion his True Vision began to grow. Arnold envisioned starring in motion pictures and having a muscular body just like his hero. In fact, Arnold was so driven after finding his True Vision that he declared at the age of thirteen, "I want to be the best-built man in the world!" His parents began to literally search through the telephone book to find a psychiatrist for their Vision-minded son.

Five years later Arnold Schwarzenegger was serving a one-year mandatory requirement in the Austrian Army. Despite the typical fifteen-hour workdays Arnold would rise early, at five in the morning, to work on his True Vision of becoming a champion bodybuilder. Exercising in the cold morning air, he was able to find both the time and energy to pursue his True Vision. Eventually he would go AWOL for a day in order to compete in the Mr. Europe contest. While he won first place, he was rewarded back at his camp with two weeks in the brig. Nothing could stand in his way, however. Arnold would do anything in order to build his body and gain knowledge of his sport. When he found that no gyms were open on Sundays he broke into one and trained until he collapsed from exhaustion.

All of his Vision-inspired work soon paid off. In 1967, at the age of twenty, Arnold was crowned the youngest Mr. Universe in history. This was only the beginning as he went on to win an unprecedented seven Mr. Olympia titles and to star in thirty-seven feature-length films, receiving up to thirty-million dollars for just one motion picture! Arnold Schwarzenegger then developed a True Vision for politics and was elected Governor of California in 2003.

Keep in mind that he began just like you and I, with nothing or very little, but formed a True Vision for his life and carried it out with dedication and persistence. Do you have a True Vision for your life? It doesn't have to be nearly as grand as Arnold's or it could be even larger, it's up to you.

Whether you would like to be debt free, smoke free, lose fifty pounds, land a promotion at work, get a new job, or even start your own business, it almost doesn't matter what you desire. You still have to work with the same success tools and the power of True Vision is sure to get you there.

The Power Of True Vision

At the very foundation of success lies the "fuel" for achievement. Without this fuel it's difficult to get off the ground. The fuel of course is True Vision, which produces the power that drives the engine of success. It's the very foundation upon which everything else is built. To begin to attempt any significant undertaking without first establishing a True Vision, is like beginning a long drive without enough gas in your car. It doesn't matter how powerful your car is, or how good a driver you are, you won't get very far. Having a True Vision can also be compared to fire, which must be hot enough to cook food or keep you warm. Your True Vision must also burn hot if any great success is to come out of it. Your Vision has to be strong and resilient, enough to see you through some rough times you encounter on the way to success. Later, I'll discuss how to develop and protect your True Vision. First, let's take a look at how images are our mind's engine fuel so that you can fully appreciate how True Vision can work for you.

The Constant Running Movie

If I ask you a simple question, such as Where are you having lunch today?, your mind will immediately create a picture, or Vision if you will. If you are having lunch at McDonald's you'll envision the golden arches and the colorful menu behind the counter. You may visualize a juicy hamburger loaded with your favorite toppings. Or, maybe you'll just picture the building, sitting there inviting you inside. Wherever you're having lunch I guarantee that you'll respond to my question by first seeing a movie in the theater of your mind.

Not only does the mind view trivial things such as where to have lunch in a vivid manner, it also thinks in pictures for important things as well. This happens day and night whether we're awake or asleep. **Consciously or unconsciously, there is a constant movie running inside your head, and you are the star.**

There was a classic study conducted at the University of Chicago many years ago involving basketball free throws. For you non-athletes, free throws (also known as foul shots) are performed by standing at a designated line on a basketball court and attempting to throw the basketball through a hoop. Three groups of high school athletes were involved in the experiment, all of equal ability. The first group was the control group, which did not practice foul shots or visualize doing them prior to the start of the experiment. The second group spent approximately one hour per day practicing their free throw shots. The third group spent time visualizing throwing successful free throws. For this group every throw went into the basket in their mental movie.

At the end of several weeks all three groups were tested. Can you guess what happened? The first group, the control group that didn't practice or visualize, showed no improvement in basketball free throws. The second group, which actually practiced free throws for one hour per day, improved the most by increasing their successful free throws by 24%. However, the real story is that the third group, which only visualized free throws and never once even picked up a basketball, came very close to equaling the winning group that actually practiced every day, by increasing their free throw success rate by 23%!

Further experimentation found, not surprisingly, that if one combines visualization with actual practice, one would surpass both the practice-only group and the visualization-only group. This is a finding that makes complete sense since it involves adding action to the thought process. However, look at how powerful the thought process is by itself. Simply visualizing every shot perfectly helped that group become almost as proficient as the group which actually practiced making their free throws!

It should come as no surprise that professional athletes use visualization techniques to enhance their game. It has been said that during his prime playing days basketball legend Michael Jordan would stand at the free throw line, close his eyes and visualize exactly how far the basket was from him, and then with his eyes still closed practice shooting free throws. Hockey great Wayne Gretzky also practiced visualization. During his active playing days he would visualize every conceivable play that could occur on the ice so that he could automatically react when in a real game. These great athletes were visualizing success. They did not waste their time thinking they were going to lose the big game that week. They visualized victory, and they achieved victory in part because of the visualization. They were not able to visualize success because they were highly paid world famous athletes. They were highly paid world famous athletes *because* they could visualize success. Vision first, victory later!

The power of the mind is truly incredible. What would happen if you applied that type of focus on your True Vision in order to improve even one aspect of your life? Practicing these techniques to cultivate your Vision at the beginning of any endeavor would make you virtually unstoppable. The power of the mind has few limitations. Whatever Vision you cultivate and believe in will ultimately materialize in your life if followed through with the appropriate action.

Da Vinci Had True Vision And More

He was a painter, sculptor, musician, engineer, architect, scientist, writer and inventor. Leonardo Da Vinci (1452–1519) believed strongly in the importance of visualization. "All of our knowledge has its origins in our perceptions. This is called pre-imaging, imagining the things that are to be," he wrote. Da Vinci's ability to visualize was so great that he actually created drawings for a helicopter, a spring-driven car, a tank, a submarine, a parachute and many other forward-thinking inventions. Four hundred years before the first automobile was invented Da Vinci envisioned it! He never limited himself to what he actually saw; instead his mind's eye saw no limits. This is a great lesson to us all. Do you look around each day and see limitations, or do you envision possibilities?

If you were alive 150 years ago and someone told you that you would be riding down the street in a horseless carriage, talking to someone 500 miles away while listening to music, how would you have reacted? Most likely you would have thought that the person was out of his mind. However, you only have to stand on any busy street corner today to see people riding in a car while talking on their cell phone, most likely with the radio turned on. The inventors of these modern conveniences had great vision not for what was, but what was to come.

I'm not asking you to look into the future and develop a True Vision for some yet-to-be invented machine. Fortunately, we don't have to have the Vision to look 150 years into the future. Nor do you need the intellect of a Leonardo Da Vinci in order to establish your own True Vision. However, in order to make improvements in your own life you must value the idea that every great invention or action is first a Vision in someone's mind. Your task is to discover your own True Vision (if you have not already done so) and develop it. You must first see yourself as a success in your own mind before it becomes a reality.

Visualize Success

All that you need to begin is the power of visualization. I want you to see yourself not as you currently are but as you would like to be. Change begins when we first create a clear picture of exactly what we want. The fact is that many people fail because they don't know exactly what they want. If you don't know where you're going, then how do you know how to get there? You don't! So, you must first have a clear desire in your mind's eye in order for that desire to manifest itself in an eventual reality. That reality is your True Vision!

You must visualize in your mind's eye having already achieved the success that you want so badly. Just like we saw with Michael Jordan and Wayne Gretzky, positive mental pictures will help drive you to achieve those positive final results. Do you want to lose weight? Since we think in pictures, not words, you would place a realistic photograph of someone about your height, age, and bone structure in strategic places throughout your home. You would make sure that you placed one where you would see it when you were most vulnerable to eating foods that you know you should stay away from. You would place one by your phone, your door, and alongside your computer screen. Again, make this photograph as detail oriented as possible. Every time you see that picture I want you to close your eyes for a few seconds and picture yourself having a similar body.

Can you "picture" this helping you? You bet it could. This is only the first thing required of you to achieve your True Vision for weight loss, but it's a good beginning. It further gives you a picture outwardly, and hopefully is at least the beginning of a True Vision in the theater of your mind as well, of what can be achieved. Now that you have the appropriate image of what you want to look like you can move further in the direction of burning that positive Vision into your mind. You must first win the battle of your own mind before your Vision becomes a reality.

Cindy Lost 85 Pounds With True Vision

When Cindy's father asked me to help his daughter, she weighed 320 pounds! She was overweight, unhappy and unhealthy. Cindy, who had not yet reached her 30th birthday, established poor eating habits as a child and had carried them into early adulthood. She desperately wanted to change but didn't know how to begin. The first thing that I wanted to do was help her see herself in a new positive way, an image that she could become. As I looked at her I thought that in her facial structure she resembled the pop singer Pink. From that point forward I made sure that she had pictures of Pink placed in strategic places around her house. I also made many references to Pink when we were together. I encouraged her to visit Pink's website and to take a close look at the facial similarities they shared. This task began to cause Cindy to look differently at herself. If she resembled Pink from the neck up, then why couldn't she look like her from the neck down as well? The possibility was there now, and very real. Sometimes when people are down and without Vision they need just one real thing to hold onto. This image was able to light a spark within Cindy, something that began to build a True Vision within her. While looking like Pink might not strike you as being a life changer, it was just the visual that Cindy needed!

Another positive mental image that stayed in Cindy's mind and helped her build and achieve her True Vision began at the supermarket. I had gone there, with a clear garbage bag in hand, to purchase sixty pounds of pure animal fat. I got some pretty strange looks as I walked through the store with my bag of fat. That evening I plopped the bag of fat down in front of Cindy (have you ever heard the sound sixty pounds of fat makes when you drop it on the floor?). She looked at it not knowing what to think at first. "There it is," I told her casually. "There is what?" Cindy asked. "It's the first sixty pounds of fat that you're going to lose. Right now you're carrying it around each day, but it won't be long until it's no longer a part of you, just like that bag of fat on the floor." I couldn't think of a better way to make this Vision real for Cindy. Sometimes the only way that we make changes in our lives is after a serious dose of reality. In Cindy's case, I wanted to give her a different way to look at her problem. I wouldn't have used this technique with everyone, but in Cindy's case I knew she needed a positive image to work toward, and a negative image to walk away from!

How many times have people launched a weight loss plan, but it was never actually real? They say they're going to lose weight, they go through the motions, they may even drop some weight in the beginning, but you know that it's just a matter of time before they fail. Why? It is because they never established a True Vision for weight loss. They could never see themselves succeeding, therefore they failed. They lacked the True Vision that must be established in order to succeed. In Cindy's case her physical likeness to Pink and the bag of fat gave her a mental picture of what she was working toward. I thought it would work very well, and it did. She was running toward something quite good, while running away from something that she no longer wanted in her life.

I then talked to Cindy about not looking at this as a diet, but a healthy lifestyle change. Someone who wants to lose weight first has to ask herself the question, "Why am I overweight?" The answer is usually eating too much of the wrong foods. Not a big revelation you might say. But here is the interesting part: the wrong foods not only cause weight gain, but are usually unhealthy as well. In Mediterranean and Asian cultures where healthier foods are consumed, we see several things. There is a much lower incidence of heart disease, cancer, stroke, and diabetes than in the United States. If we look at the problem this way it's obvious that eating healthier, more nutritious foods not only causes weight loss, but will also have a direct effect on how long you live, and on the many good years of health you enjoy as well! This is one area where you really can have it all: you can look well, be healthy and feel good. Why would you want your life to be any other way?

Looking at nutrition this way can change your perception of why you need to eat healthier foods as opposed to eating the typical American diet. Eating in a way that will improve your health, increase your longevity, and give you more energy to enjoy life has many obvious benefits. These include the amount and quality of time that you can spend with family and friends and the increase in energy for your job. In short, eating right will make your entire life more full and enjoyable. Isn't this better than just looking at this as one more diet? And it's actually far more accurate isn't it?

Over the next several months and with much hard work Cindy lost 85 pounds! She felt better, was healthier, more attractive, and she gained an amazing amount of confidence. The "Pink" inside of her could finally shine through.

The first rule of success is to have a True Vision that burns like a hot fire. This is the driving force that carried Cindy forward to success. It is the driving force that allows each person to fulfill his, or her, own destiny a force that each of us can harness regardless of our past failures, educational level, or background. Let's discuss the steps involved in making your True Vision a reality in the next chapter.

chapter two

CREATE YOUR OWN TRUE VISION

*You start with a vision and it manifests
in its own interesting fashion.*
     —Lois Trombely

It's Time To Create Your Own True Vision

What is it that you want to achieve? I've found that even in the happiest, most successful people there is something more that they want to do with their life. Sometimes it's obvious. Maybe the doctor said that if you don't lose weight you're headed for serious medical problems. With others it's less obvious. I have an acquaintance who is still trying to find his career path and he's more than forty years old. For those of you who have not yet developed a True Vision for any particular path in life, I would suggest that you find some time during the day for "Vision practice" to determine exactly what you want to accomplish. This isn't as difficult as you might think. Actually, you might not have given it as much of the *right* kind of thought as needed. You may have worried about it and projected negative images in your mind's eye regarding your future (remember that constantly running movie in the theater of your mind?). However, you've probably never truly understood what you need to do in order to discover the real Vision that lies buried beneath the surface of worry. For those of you who know exactly what your True Vision is you can skip the following sequence. Then again you may not want to skip it. Perhaps there is an additional Vision waiting to be discovered? Maybe you're only getting a mere glimpse of certain pictures in your mind and you're not able to develop them. Maybe you do have that one burning Vision but for some reason it's just not matching your current reality. If this is the case, read on.

First, make sure you're in a place where you will not be disturbed. Now take out a pen or pencil and a few sheets of paper. Any sort of paper will do. I've planned entire sales campaigns on the back of discarded envelopes. So, don't nit-pick the process. If you're more comfortable in front of your computer, that's okay too. Many people fail because they're always looking for that perfect beginning, that pristine moment when the stars align perfectly in order to give them that special inspiration to get started. Well, guess what? That moment is not coming, and if you continue to wait for everything to be just right before you begin this process, the opportunity will be lost. Don't be like the person who wants to change his life but is waiting to begin "the first of the year" or "right after the weather clears up" or "just as soon as lady luck smiles on him." There will always be an excuse not to begin because life is never going to be perfect. Ask yourself this: how has procrastinating worked out for you so far? It's time to get started today, right now while you're reading these words. Go to that calendar on your wall or desk and mark today as the day that you began to take control of that one thing you've left undone, that one unfulfilled Vision. Let this be the moment that you begin your success journey towards creating and then accomplishing your ultimate True Vision.

Let's Get Started

Begin by making a list of all the things that you're proud of in your life. This can be anything from having a good marriage and being proud of your children, to achieving a promotion at work, or having gotten good grades in school. Write freely regarding your accomplishments; add anything that comes to mind. Keep writing, regardless of how many you have listed, until you finally run out. Perhaps this list is short. Cheer up! That's why you're reading this book. It doesn't matter what happened in your past or what's happening in your present. It's tomorrow that we're working on, and your tomorrow can be anything that you want it to be when you have True Vision!

When you've completed writing your list of past accomplishments, it's time to begin a new list. Let's call this second list "future accomplishments." It might be made up of some things that you've either never done or tried to do and failed. As this list may be a little more difficult than the first, I want you to take more care in making it. It is also the list where you write down your desires, things that you are interested in pursuing. Maybe you've never parachuted out of an airplane. Do you want to? Do you see yourself doing it? Do you have a True Vision for this particular challenge? Then list it! My point is, keep this list as true to yourself as possible. You may already have an idea that it is identifying a career that you wish to focus on. If this is the case then keep the list focused on potential careers. As I've already stated, if you have that one burning desire that you must absolutely accomplish, then you don't really need to do this list. You already have something of a Vision, now all you have to do is develop it.

Once your list is complete it's time to reflect upon each item on your list and begin to visualize yourself doing the actual act you have listed. For example, let's imagine that you placed on your list: attend law school. I want you to take a few minutes and visualize yourself, as realistically as possible, attending classes and studying late at night. Picture yourself practicing in a court of law. How does it look? Is it easy to imagine? Now ask yourself is the Vision strong? How does it feel? Try to visualize the sacrifices involved as well as the benefits.

Continue to look inside yourself. Take a look at your past accomplishments list. What sort of attributes did it take to achieve what you have already accomplished? You need to employ those same qualities and use them to achieve even more. For example, if you have already displayed a strong desire to take reasonable risks and love high places, then parachuting out of an airplane is probably something that you can visualize yourself doing. Or, perhaps you are someone who has been a dependable friend to people in time of hardship and need. Perhaps you've listed on your past accomplishments list that you are a good friend, active parent, or relationship builder. These very same attributes could serve you well in social work, psychology, or police work. Maybe you could end up writing an advice column for your local newspaper, or start an advice newsletter or Internet blog. If the ability is there and your past accomplishments list validates it, then it should be visualized and transferred in some way onto your future accomplishments list. This exercise will help bring your True Vision into clear focus.

It's much easier to find your True Vision for something new if these are skills which in some form appeared on your accomplishments list. For instance, if you have shown yourself to be open, friendly, gregarious, comfortable meeting new people, and usually make a great first impression, then maybe a high-powered sales position should be on your list. What's notable here is that you wouldn't need to have listed a sales position in your past accomplishments list. All you would need to have shown is a tendency toward abilities or qualities a sales position might require. These skills may have shown themselves in another part of your life. Maybe you're the person that everyone calls to get together for social events? You may have listed this on your past accomplishments list as "a happy social life." I know of someone who falls into this category. In fact, he is so well liked that he has been asked to be best man by nine different grooms! Now there's a person who should be in sales of some sort, and he is. Or, maybe you're the one who organizes everyone for social events. You are a doer, you are a planner, and you are highly organized. What career paths might you visualize based on these proven skills?

I believe that each of us was born with certain abilities, and that it's just a matter of finding and developing them. With some people it's obvious: the child who is able to play a perfect piano concerto at the age of six, the strong, naturally coordinated, well-muscled teenager who wants to play football. Please don't put "play professional basketball" on your future accomplishments list if you're 5'3" and have never played the game. Look for those distinguishing characteristics that separate you from someone else, however subtle they may be. And trust in the simple truth: like virtually everyone else, your distinguishing characteristics have already shown up in an activity, or in some part of your life. As you break down and carefully analyze your past accomplishments list you'll see them.

For those of you who are looking at other parts of your lives, instead of a career, the same process applies. Maybe you're interested in improving your personal relationships. Your past accomplishments list will include relationships that have been successful. You will then be able to create a Vision of success by using past positive relationships, and determine what made those relationships successful. For example, if you've cultivated a positive relationship with your sister, ask yourself why. Is it the fact that you spend time together and simply try hard at making that particular relationship work? Or, is the strength of your relationship based upon the balance between your differing personality types? Perhaps you're more outgoing and she is naturally shy. Whatever the reason, I'm asking you to visualize the use of those characteristics with which you already have had success.

Modeling Success Traits

If you don't have any real successes in your background and are having a difficult time listing previous success traits don't let that bother you. Use your imagination instead. What would you like to accomplish? You can actively copy or model another person's successful traits. You simply copy traits that others have had success with in their life in order to help build your own True Vision.

The modeling theory states that if you can appropriately copy someone who is successful in the same area that you're interested in improving, then you too will be a success. There is a lot of merit in this approach. While it's easier to carry over your own success traits into another area of your life, modeling another person's successful behavior can work too. For example, if you developed a True Vision and wish to become the best salesperson at your company, you would actively copy the success traits of the current best salesperson at your company. Start with how he dresses, and proceed to his physical mannerisms. How does this person shake hands? Does he always pat people on the back? Does he stand with arms folded, or hands at his sides relaxed? Take a good look at how such salespeople present themselves during a sales call, in front of a customer. What can you model from their actual presentation? Focus on how they operate and exactly what makes them successful.

If the lead salesperson for your company tends to dress more formally and smiles a great deal, you do the same. If she makes twenty "cold calls" per day and takes a client out to lunch every day, you do the same thing. When you model someone's success traits you're putting yourself in a position to succeed. The theory is what works for one will work for another, so long as you're actually modeling all, or most, of the important traits that successful person has. It's easy to smile more or dress in a certain way, but that may not be enough. If the successful person arrives at work one hour early each day or stays late one hour every other night in order to get a head start on the next day, you have to do the same thing. Don't pick and choose or attempt to model only things that are not challenging. You must be modeling and blending into your own workday as many aspects you can identify as possible in order for you to achieve what Ms. or Mr. Success has achieved.

I remember Clark, a supervisor, who was in charge of six of my stores. He mentioned in a meeting that it seemed that no matter how hard he tried he just could not beat John, who was one of his rivals for Supervisor of the Month. Month after month he came in a disappointing third or fourth. I discussed modeling John's most successful traits. At first Clark opposed the idea. "You want me to copy him?" Clark asked incredulously. "Not exactly," I replied. The human ego can sometimes be a fragile thing. Some people refuse to give credit to others because doing so somehow threatens their own self-esteem. How can someone who resents another actually model that person's behavior? Did you ever notice that when someone else succeeds in a big way it's easy for some to attribute it to luck, or some sort of special circumstance? However, when *he* does well, it is due to hard work, and nothing more. Funny isn't it? I had to convince Clark that not only was John successful because he was good at his job, but Clark would also be better off if he, too, in fact modeled those same success traits.

I went on to explain that there are reasons why some people succeed and others do not. Part of that is working smart. If someone works just as hard but continues to lose, then he or she might be working hard but not smart. John was in fact doing things that were helping him achieve success. He would not only speak to his managers daily, but also say the right things at the right time. For example, you can tell someone working for you that you want them to increase their sales, but did you give them specific ideas on how to do it? The poor supervisor might say, "Raise your sales or you're fired." That's not supervising at all. A good supervisor is part cheerleader, part conveyor of information, part teacher and part big brother or sister. Nowhere is he or she part intimidator. I explained to Clark that modeling might very well help him work smarter and give him that extra something that he'd been lacking.

If you want to make a new doorway in one of your walls, you can take a few steps back and run as hard as you can into the wall with your head as many times as possible before you render yourself unconscious. No one can question the effort that you're putting into the job. You're working hard all right, no doubt. The question is, are you working smart? I think the answer is pretty obvious.

Let's say there are ten major reasons why John is our most successful supervisor. These ten reasons comprise almost one hundred percent of the reason for his great success. If you're currently working at an acceptable level, chances are you're already performing many of these success traits but perhaps not performing them with a high level of intensity. Your performance may also be missing two or three of the most important success traits, the ones that put the other guy over the top.

After several meetings and some salesmanship of my own, I got Clark to try these modeling techniques. Within two months Clark finished a close second to John for Supervisor of the Month. On the fourth month Clark actually did it—he beat John for Supervisor of the Month. An intense rivalry ensued with both men achieving greater financial success than either ever imagined. It was just a matter of Clark finding what he needed to do to make this work, and then doing it. **Isn't that how success is ultimately achieved? Visualizing what works, going out and actually doing it, and then in a disciplined manner repeating that behavior. This is called working smart, not just hard!**

Keep in mind that you're still a unique individual, and no amount of modeling can replace your one-of-a-kind personality. You'll bring some qualities to your career that the person whom you're modeling will not have. One of these qualities could easily send you to the top of your profession. Once you begin to achieve some success you'll be able to refine your best traits by bringing more of your own personality into the mix, thereby truly owning your newfound abilities. No matter how many new success traits you model, you'll still maintain your unique individuality.

Your Very Personal True Vision

In creating your own True Vision you're in essence creating something that is unique and personal to you. Maybe your True Vision is to lose forty pounds, to stop smoking, or to get out of debt. Whatever it is, it must be something that is yours. You must own it. It must suit you! You'll want to exercise your own unique God-given abilities to become all that you are capable of being, growing in your chosen direction. To find, and bring to fruition, your own True Vision.

Fortunately, whatever your desire might be, the rules of success are the same. You must begin with a Vision, and in the beginning the best way to turn your True Vision into a reality is to continuously run that success film over and over again on your own personal movie screen, in the theater of the mind. If you have a strong True Vision and you can visualize in detail your success, how you'll get there, when you'll get there, why you want to get there, and who will help you get there, and you truly believe it, you will be able to achieve it! There are Vision Steps that will be discussed later in the book, which will further help you on your path to success!

If you're a skeptic you may not quite buy into the power of visualization, or the need for building a True Vision. I've heard this before from a few others, and I try to explain that visualization techniques via the theater of the mind has worked for me for every success that I've ever had, and can work for you. It's almost like programming a computer. You don't realize a positive end result until you have the proper program in place. It's a process that also engages the subconscious mind. We must first program that mental movie of success. As the psychologist William James put it a century ago: "There is a law in psychology that if you form a picture in your mind of what you would like to be, and you keep and hold that picture there long enough, you will soon become exactly as you have been thinking."

I was first recognized by GUINNESS WORLD RECORDS for setting a chin-up record in 2006. A short time later, another individual broke my record. As soon as I heard about that I immediately developed a True Vision for reclaiming the top spot. Not only did I see myself once again winning a GUINNESS WORLD RECORDS record for chin-ups, but I felt that I could also do something completely different: I would break two world records on the same morning! I began training for what I feel is one of the most difficult movements, the Squat Thrust. On the morning of February 7, 2007 I was again recognized by GUINNESS WORLD RECORDS, this time for both chin-ups and squat thrusts.

What I did on that day was to fulfill my True Vision for breaking two records on the same morning. However, I believe that what I accomplished could also be done by any person in good health who has a True Vision for such events. **The most important point, one that I really want you to understand, is that having a True Vision, and visualizing yourself achieving that mental movie, is the beginning of what it takes to get what you want.**

I can recall falling asleep in bed each night visualizing myself performing every aspect of each of the 44 chin-ups! From how tight I would squeeze the bar and how my body would feel being hoisted up and down each time, to how my chin would feel touching the cold steel bar 44 times. While I had never once performed 44 chin-ups in practice, I knew that I had to first exceed the previous GUINNESS WORLD RECORDS record in my mind before it could become a reality. While I am not a professional athlete, I still used the same techniques these professionals practice regularly. One thing visualization does is make the thing you want to accomplish become more credible, more achievable to you as you see it happening on a regular basis in the mind. This technique will work for you regardless of your current position in life. I have no special ability beyond what I believe that I can do, and if I can do this, so can you!

Great Athletes, Entertainers And Scientists Visualize Success

The technique of visualization has also worked for many others. Here are just a few:

Olympic swimming multiple gold medalist Michael Phelps visualized standing on the center podium with the gold medal around his neck. He visualized what winning all of those gold medals would look and feel like.

Perhaps the greatest golfer who ever played the game, Jack Nicklaus, has observed: "I never hit a shot, not even in practice, without having a very sharp in-focus picture of it in my head. It's like a color movie. First I see the ball where I want it to finish, nice and white, sitting up high on the bright green grass. Then the scene quickly changes and I 'see' the ball going there; its path, trajectory and shape, even its behavior on landing. Then there is sort of a fade out, and the next scene shows me making the kind of swing that will turn the images into reality on landing. Finally, I see myself making the kind of swing that will turn the first two images into reality. These 'home movies' are a key to my concentration."*

Mixed martial arts champion Sean Sherk had this to say about visualization in an interview: "I visualize before a fight by putting myself in different situations mentally. Whatever my opponent's going to do to me—escaping mounts, avoiding takedowns, boxing, so I visualize that type of stuff as well. I think for the most part visualization is good for training the mind. You train the body to do all this stuff

*Reprinted with the permission of Simon & Schuster, Inc., from *Golf My Way* by Jack Nicklaus. Copyright © 1974 by Jack Nicklaus. All rights reserved.

and I think it's good to train the mind as well [by] using repetition in your head."

Wayne Gretzky believes if you visualize yourself doing something, you can make that image come true. He said that he must have rehearsed holding the Stanley Cup ten thousand times, and when it subsequently came true it was like an electric bolt had gone up his spine.

Actor and martial arts expert Bruce Lee committed to paper his Vision:

"My definite chief aim: I, Bruce Lee, will be the highest paid Oriental superstar in the United States. In return I will give the most exciting performances and render the best of quality in the capacity of an actor. Starting 1970 I will achieve world fame and from then onward till the end of 1980 I will have in my possession $10,000,000. I will live the way I please and achieve inner harmony and happiness. Bruce Lee Jan. 1969." Lee went on to achieve fame and fortune as a top martial arts action star!

In a story reported a few years ago actor Jim Carrey, when he was still a struggling comic and washing dishes part-time, wrote a check to himself for $10,000,000. He dated it November 1995, and tucked it away in his wallet. In the fall of 1995 he signed a $10,000,000 contract to film The Mask. Carrey is now one of the biggest stars in Hollywood. Having a True Vision for success begins first in the theater of the mind and manifests itself through working hard and working smart until that success is achieved.

Finally, consider this. Between 1956 and 1980, the former Soviet Union was virtually untouchable in Olympic gymnastics. During that exact time frame, the Soviet coaches engaged in visualization techniques to help their gymnasts and it worked quite well bringing them more gold medals in this sport than any other country!

Fortunately, creating a True Vision through visualization is certainly not limited to famous entertainers and athletes. Dr. O. Carl Simonton, a radiologist and respected cancer specialist who was honored by the American Medical Association for his film *Affirmations For Getting Well*, has done a great amount of research in the area of using visualization techniques with cancer patients. A pilot study he conducted from 1974 to 1981 demonstrated an increase in survival time and improvement in quality of life in patients who practiced visualization. His early research established the foundation for two widely acclaimed books which he co-authored, *Getting Well Again* and *The Healing Journey*, works that have been utilized by many to help them build their own True Vision of success over disease.

Cancer survivor Ole Nielsen Schou recently told his story in a *Forbes* magazine article entitled "Miracle Survivors." In it Schou told of the day he found out his melanoma had spread to his liver, abdomen, lungs, bones and ten spots in his brain. This was certainly dire news for this gentleman. While surgeons removed the abdominal tumor, they did not treat his other tumors. Ole, however, used a form of positive visualization to try and overcome his disease. Imagining his metastases were rats, he visualized chasing them with a club. When he returned for another scan four months later it was found that 90% of his tumors had melted away, and soon they were completely gone!

Some would call the story unbelievable, and certainly I am not recommending that any patient stop their regular treatments and concentrate solely on this technique; that would be foolhardy. However, what would be wrong with adding some positive visualization techniques to one's normal therapy? Putting forth a positive running mental movie is the first step in achieving success regardless of what your desire might be!

You are now in possession of a technique that athletes, entertainers and scientists use to help themselves and others. What will you do with this powerful information? Will you toss it aside, disregarding the many benefits that can come from using this information? Will you continue to attribute others success to luck, circumstances or connections? Or, will you see the tremendous opportunity that you have to change your life for the better by developing a True Vision?

Keep in mind that your True Vision is not a gimmick, and it is certainly not a dream. My definition of a dream is something that you wish for but have no real chance of obtaining: a fleeting fancy of the mind, something that would be nice, but something that you know in your heart will never happen, like wishing to win the lottery. **On the other hand, your True Vision is a positive, vivid mental movie of exactly what you want to achieve, right down to the smallest details. And it's based on concrete evidence gleaned from what you've already achieved, are able to achieve by certain traits that you've demonstrated in other activities, or may achieve by successfully modeling someone else.** The difference between a mere dream and a True Vision is the difference between fantasy and fact. There is literally no comparison. Whatever your True Vision might be, know that it has meaning, it has power; it has captured your imagination and you are going to achieve it!

Reinforcing Your True Vision (Vision Building)

I want you to spend some time each day burning your True Vision into your subconscious. This is the part of your brain that never rests, working around the clock 24 hours a day, seven days per week. I want you to picture yourself actively performing your Vision. As I've stated previously, we think in pictures not words. Those images are stored in the subconscious mind. As Napoleon Hill writes in *Think and Grow Rich*: "The subconscious mind is the connecting link between the finite mind of man and Infinite Intelligence." It is now time to tap into that part of your brain that, up to now, has not been utilized to its fullest.

Follow these steps:

1. See a vivid movie of you succeeding at whatever you're doing. Run the movie of yourself (not just a picture) achieving your Vision, the more realistic the better. What are you wearing? Who is with you? Who are the people that will be impressed with your success? Where will this take place? When will this happen? Who else is involved with helping you achieve your success?

2. Try to see and feel all of the details. Remember how I could actually feel my chin touching the bar on my way to being recognized by GUINNESS WORLD RECORDS? Try to include every detail that you can think of in your Vision. Reality is in the details, so make sure that you are as detailed as possible when you practice your visualization.

3. Make sure to actually feel the emotion that goes along with succeeding at your True Vision. I want your heart to beat a little faster; I want your palms to get a little sweaty. I want you to know how it's going to feel when you achieve your True Vision.

I call this "Vision building," which can be accomplished while relaxing or watching television. You can Vision build any time that your attention is not fully needed elsewhere. For example, never Vision build when driving a car or any time your focus is needed on something of importance. I want you to completely concentrate on these

Vision building sessions which will take your full attention! The more time that you spend building your Vision the stronger it will be and the more power you will have in actually causing it to come to fruition. The more you see and believe in your True Vision, the better your opportunity to accomplish it.

Use Negative Pictures To Achieve A Positive Vision

If you have a smoke free Vision, then make sure that you see yourself as a non-smoker. Picture yourself smoke free. Visualize daily that you're having great success in this area. Picture having clear pink lungs and being able to breathe freely. Picture yourself not being so easily winded, and your home, car, and clothing free of that stale nasty smell. Sometimes negative visualization may work effectively too— remember the sixty pounds of fat that I placed in a clear garbage bag to give to Cindy? If you are a smoker, a mental image of yourself gasping for air in a hospital bed can be an inspiring way to fulfill your True Vision of quitting. While I prefer to visualize positive images as a way to propel you toward your True Vision, we sometimes do things to *avoid* an outcome rather than to gain a certain result. In other words, you can run towards something attractive or away from something harmful or grotesque. As long as we propel ourselves in the proper direction it doesn't matter whether we're doing it to get closer to something or away from something else.

Kendra's True Vision

Kendra was 31 years old and she had smoked steadily since the age of 13. At one point her habit reached one and a half packs a day. She had tried patches, chewing gum, and going cold turkey. She occasionally stopped smoking for a few weeks at a time, but always failed to make it all the way, and became frustrated as her victories were temporary. She had tried to quit and failed a dozen times.

When Kendra asked me to help, the first thing I wanted to do was to learn more about her and to get an idea of why she smoked. As I got to know her I realized that painting a picture of how great she would feel smoke free would not be as effective as drawing vivid mental pictures of black diseased lungs. She needed a jolt of reality so I told her stories of those who traveled the same road that she was headed down who were now either dead or dying. I related in detail how someone with emphysema spends his or her final days gasping for air tied to various tubes for prolonged periods of time. Most important, Kendra has a young child, so I reinforced my negative picture of her future by giving her an image of this child standing by her bedside crying as he watched his mother dying a slow painful death.

Admittedly the picture I created for Kendra's mental movie was not pretty. I would have daily conversations with her to reinforce the negative imagery and even introduced her to an individual who wheezed and clamored for air by merely standing up and attempting to walk across a small room. When Kendra was at home, she was further instructed to focus on these negative mental images. Each day when I saw her I would ask, "Did you smoke a cigarette today?" And week by week, as the negative mental picture intensified, her fear intensified as well, and consequently her smoking slowly decreased. She wanted to get as far away as possible from those frightening images. Kendra eventually achieved her True Vision for a smoke free life by trying to avoid a horrific future!

While it didn't happen overnight, Kendra slowly began to see herself as a non-smoker. We had long talks about how good she would feel as a non-smoker. I gave her positive images of good health and more energy, something to work toward as she ran away from the negative. When her True Vision of being a non-smoker was soundly established it was only a matter of time before she was in fact smoke free. As of this writing Kendra has been smoke free for eight years! When you establish a True Vision, for whatever reason, it's only a matter of time before it becomes a reality.

If you are going to use a negative image to help reinforce your positive True Vision then I suggest that you obtain a picture of how someone looks who is suffering from lung cancer. You may also find a picture of how the lungs look after so many years of smoking. Then place the photos in an area where you are most tempted to smoke. This may be in your car or at the office. In some cases it may be wise putting these pictures in your pocket and looking at them three times a day for up to one minute. I would even encourage you to visit those who are interned in a hospital bed, tied to tubes and gasping for breath because of their habit.

All of this may seem rather brutal; however, if you are a smoker, have you been able to make a permanent change so far? Have you been able to establish a True Vision without the use of these techniques? You need to reinforce the fact that you are smoke free. Perhaps your True Vision of a smokeless life is only going to become a reality if you can actually see what will occur if change is not made. People in general are survivors. One reason that you may smoke is that you don't really believe that anything bad is ever going to happen to you. You've been smoking for a certain number of years and nothing bad has happened to you yet. You're convinced that cancer, emphysema and heart disease are what happen to other people. That's why you have to be reminded of all of the negative consequences of your current actions. Being constantly reminded, in as graphic a way as possible, that smoking is harmful to your health, will cut your life short, and will eventually cause pain to you and your entire family is the reality check you need to take action! I want that image of a smoke free you to be reinforced any way possible on a daily basis. I want you to run away from those awful images, and run toward a positive new you. I want you to get to the point where you know you're not going to smoke again. It's not a wish, or a dream, but a True Vision that turns into your reality!

Remember, you will never be able to achieve what you cannot first envision yourself achieving. If you learn one thing from this book let it be that (but I sure hope you learn more). Our goal in the very beginning must be to increase the size, scope, and intensity of your Vision. You will always gravitate toward your most burning desire, that one constant movie that plays non-stop in the theater of the mind. You must see yourself as a non-smoker, someone who is at the ideal weight, or a person who is debt free—or whatever your Vision might be. The new you is working on a plan to succeed at whatever you feel will make you a happier, healthier person. The new you has your very own True Vision!

Whatever your True Vision might be, I want you to burn it into your brain. Eat it, drink it, live it! Consume yourself fully with the notion that you will in fact become whatever your True Vision dictates. At first you may feel like a fake, like you're fooling yourself, as the Vision may be somewhat weak. However, you build a Vision the same way that you build a house, with a good strong foundation, and then one board and one nail at a time. At first it may not look much like a house; however, if you keep building you will eventually have a home that will provide you with warmth, shelter, and happy memories. The same can be said for your True Vision. You may not feel like you're going to achieve this in the beginning, but keep in mind that you're learning something new. Like playing the piano or skiing, it takes a little time to perfect your new skill. You have over 100 billion neurons (nerve cells) in the brain that continuously send and receive signals between the brain and nervous system. You're making new connections or synapses all the time. That is one reason why old negative thought patterns can be broken, and replaced by new positive ones. The key is to keep at it. Soon you'll have a strong Vision that will become a reality providing you with a better life, a sense of great accomplishment, and leading you to other victories. It all begins with that one True Vision!

Ending Mental Myopia

If you're having a difficult time establishing your True Vision, you might be suffering from "mental myopia." This occurs when your mental movie is playing the wrong script. You may consciously desire to lose forty pounds, or to quit smoking, but your inner movie keeps playing the version where you fail. Or worse yet, you don't even begin (keep in mind if you never begin you have already failed). Is this happening to you? If it is, think about it as just an old habit that is dying hard. Whenever this negativity creeps into your psyche deal with it gently and you will diffuse it. Don't let it frustrate you. Smile to yourself and think, "That was the old script; it's time now to play the new one." Then move directly to the positive Vision you have established for yourself. If you're having a problem developing your True Vision, know that in the beginning it will seem like you're constantly changing the script of your mental movie. Readjusting your mental movie is all part of the learning process in the beginning.

In some cases the absence of confidence is so great that each time you attempt to create your new Vision of success you're met with negative thoughts of defeat. If this happens then back off a little. It may be that you're mentally creating too much for you to believe. Start with a smaller Vision, one that feels more attainable and less paralyzing. For example, if you're attempting to gain a True Vision for losing forty pounds but have a difficult time seeing yourself at that weight, picture yourself at a weight that is only ten or twenty pounds lighter than you are now. Whatever positive mental image of success you can see and believe is the one that's right for you. Your Vision can always be increased as success is achieved. I'm not asking you to change your desire to ultimately lose forty pounds, just begin with a Vision of losing ten pounds if that's easier to visualize.

Once you begin to establish these positive pictures, as the weeks pass you'll find that your new Vision gets more and more mental airtime as the old failure pictures diminish and lose their punch. Instead of having to counteract the negative outdated mental pictures, you'll find that they will begin to fade into the past until they have absolutely no power over your new positive True Vision!

Isn't it time to create a positive reality? You may have desired a change in your life for quite a while. Ask yourself this: If not now, when? How many more days are you going to let slip past before you develop a True Vision for your life? Why not act now? If there's something in your life that you know needs attention, you will soon have all the tools to deal with it. There may not be a need for you to search out your True Vision. Your True Vision may be a change that's necessary and it is there in front of you, a part of your life, staring you in the face each day. It may be causing you and your family pain and worry, preventing you from having the sort of life that you really want. As I write these words, I have no idea what your True Vision should be. I do know that whatever you have in your life that's holding you back, stopping you from being the sort of person that you've always wanted to be, *can* be eliminated. I can also tell you with complete confidence that when you establish a True Vision to deal with the problem you will already be on your way to success. You, too, can be like the many others that have created their own victories by first establishing a True Vision of exactly what they wanted from life.

Years Of Abuse Erased With True Vision

Peter was a successful fifty-year old business success, happily married and the father of three. Unfortunately, his prospects for a healthy future were in doubt. Peter was thirty pounds overweight and, more importantly, he suffered from a heart condition known as cardiomyopathy. Among Peter's problems were the following: that he ate the wrong foods, smoked, and was a heavy consumer of both alcohol and coffee. While Peter had everything to live for, there was a good chance that he would die too soon, a victim of his many reckless habits.

Peter asked me to assist him; he had established his True Vision by coming to the realization that he wanted the best years of his life to still be ahead of, not behind, him. Whether it was through fear or a longing to just feel good again, Peter visualized what he wanted to look and feel like. It was a strong True Vision and would not be denied! While Peter had never been an athlete or possessed any particular athletic ability, I designed a fitness and diet program for him, which he practiced regularly. It changed everything for him.

I want you to understand a very important point: Peter hated to exercise. In fact, I don't think that there are many people that I've met through the years that actually despised exercise as much as Peter did, but he did it anyway. **It is in doing the things that we don't want to do that we not only learn Self-Discipline but also begin to understand how a True Vision is realized.** Without a strong and growing True Vision there can be no long-term Self-Discipline (more on that later).

Even though Peter had abused his body terribly, and at fifty years of age would surely not be considered a kid, he made stunning progress. He lost the entire thirty pounds in less than four months. (Incidentally, it is a crucial point that weight gained gradually should be removed gradually). What is more amazing is that Peter no longer had a heart issue! Thirty years of abuse was virtually erased in four months! How? Because Peter had a True Vision of himself as a lean healthy person with the best years of his life still ahead of him and then acted on that Vision. Today, Peter plays racquetball, tennis, jogs and bikes. The active life he leads has positively impacted his wife and children, too, as they enjoy an outdoor lifestyle together, as a family—to Peter, the greatest blessing of them all.

What are you waiting for? Do you need to lose weight? Quit smoking? Increase your income? Like Peter, you may already have a True Vision and have no need to complete all of the steps we've talked about in this chapter. Your problem may be how to keep your True Vision flourishing so that it will ultimately become your reality.

chapter three

A STRONG TRUE VISION

Visualize this thing you want.
See it, feel it, believe in it.
Make your mental blueprint and begin.
    —Robert Collier

Keep The Vision Strong And Growing

Congratulations! You now have a True Vision for the future. However, just like any other entity, it must either grow or die, because nothing stays the same. The universe is constantly in flux, and so is your life. You're in constant motion. It's just a matter of which direction you choose to move in. Ask yourself, are you moving forward, or falling behind? Growing richer, or getting poorer? Cultivating better relationships, or further isolating yourself from people who could better your life? Achieving a stronger healthier body, or falling into poor physical condition? Increasing your intelligence or allowing it to disintegrate? Growing closer to God, or taking one step back each day? You must actively pursue whatever is important in your life on an almost daily basis. If you don't you will find that your act of omission, even if unintentional, will, like a wave, push you further away from it.

How many people set out to gain thirty or forty pounds of fat? I can't think of one person. They have just failed to establish a True Vision of being at their desired weight. Likewise, how many of us wake up one day and proclaim, "Today is the day that I begin a lifelong smoking habit that will ultimately give me poor health, and cut my life short?" You guessed it, none of us.

However, if as a young adult you don't have an active True Vision of a smoke-free life then you may very well end up as a smoker. Put in plain terms, those who don't know where they're going may end up anywhere. *Always be actively moving toward your Vision.* I remind you once again, if you're not moving toward something, then you're moving away from it, as life constantly changes for either the good or the bad.

Charles Dickens wrote, "The mine which time has slowly dug beneath familiar objects is sprung in an instant, and what was rock before, becomes but sand and dust." The same can be said for your True Vision. It is alive and well if it's growing. Or it can die if it sits dormant long. So, how do you keep the Vision strong and growing?

Help Your Vision Grow Through The Use Of A Journal

You may stoke your Vision to keep it hot by putting your thoughts down on paper. Think about your weekly or monthly activities. What worked for you? What failed? What will you do with the first "real" money that you make? (Don't build a big house in a small town; I've found that some people really hate that). In general, keep the Vision active and in your mind's eye every chance you get. Keeping a daily, weekly, or monthly journal will give your True Vision a life of its own, one that is much needed. This is because there are so many things that come at us in the course of a day, so many diversions, that it's easy for a small flame to be extinguished. You have to stay focused on what is important to you!

When we write something down we simultaneously give it legitimacy. The printed word has the power to influence you. It can impact your life in ways that you may not realize or appreciate. Be your own reporter, and record all of your positive thoughts and efforts regarding your True Vision. Write down all of the details. If you had a meeting with your immediate supervisor, write about the ideas that you suggested and the response you received. Further, write about who was at the meeting, and some of the more important things that they said. Write down your impressions of the various people in attendance. Who seemed hostile to your ideas? Who seemed to welcome them with open arms? Did you behave in a manner that would warrant the promotion that your Vision is centered around? What could you have done differently?

If your True Vision is weight loss, write down all of the things that will help you succeed. When you weigh yourself and find that you've lost even two pounds, write a note about what foods you have been eating over the previous few days. Your body is going to react differently to certain foods than another person's body. While we all have more in common than not, we each have certain subtleties in our personalities that can make a big difference when manipulated to our advantage. However, we won't know what works if we don't keep an active journal. The journal will also keep you in touch with your own feelings about the pursuit of your True Vision. This is important. You need to analyze your quest introspectively in order to understand why you are doing what you are doing.

Always try to finish every journal entry with a positive line or two concerning your will to carry through and make your Vision a reality. This is called an Affirmation Reminder. (I'll talk more about that technique later in the book). We do this to further drive into our psyche the reality of what we're going to accomplish. For example, your closing lines may read like this: "I am more ready now than ever before to continue my fight for that new position. I'll give the boss no choice but to pick me it will be so obvious." Or, if your journal entry involves weight loss: "I avoided eating a dessert for six days in a row. That adds up to about three thousand calories saved! I'm on my way." You might even write something more emotional. Write whatever moves you and helps you to stay the course.

The following was taken directly from a journal entry that I made during the second year of my first big company's existence. At the time, I was seeking bank financing to open my next few stores. Unfortunately, I could not convince any banker of the merits of loaning money to my fledgling startup. My journal entry is very descriptive regarding this fact: "I have now been turned down by twelve banks! Well, the others better get ready because before I'm finished I'm going to visit one hundred banks! I will get a loan and this idea will grow. PERIOD!" Incidentally, I didn't have to go to one hundred banks. I got the money that I needed to take my business to the next level on my thirty-third try! I went to thirty-three banks before I got the loan that was so badly needed to grow my company. I was in fact so shocked when the banker said yes that I just stared at him for several seconds before saying, "Are you sure you want to do this? No one else seems to think it's a good idea." I was smooth wasn't I?

Would I have had the persistence to solicit thirty-three banks if I didn't write in my journal that I was prepared to go to one hundred? Of course not! As you can see, your final affirmation should be a positive one, written with as much passion as you can muster. Remember, the stronger your True Vision the greater the heat it will produce. The bigger and hotter the fire, the harder it is to extinguish. This will be useful later on no matter what your Vision entails. Whether you write in your journal every day or weekly, make sure that you begin and continue on with this most important method in fanning the Vision flame. The written word is a powerful tool that can help solidify your Vision by giving it its own identity and much needed credibility, especially in the early going. Your words fan the Vision flame.

One more reason to keep an active journal (as if you needed another reason), is that when you're writing you tend to organize your thoughts. Writing forces you to see yourself more clearly and consequently become more deliberate regarding the actions you are taking during your quest to realize your Vision. When we think in a more orderly fashion we tend to be able to relay our thoughts better verbally as well. We can therefore communicate better, produce more, and be happier with our final product, whatever that may be. Some people use the excuse that they are horrible at spelling to stop them from keeping a journal. Or, maybe they were never good writers in school so they avoid the task of writing down their thoughts. Don't let this happen to you. This is your journal, and no one else has to see it. Don't worry about your handwriting, typing, or spelling skills. These things are unimportant compared to fostering the growth of your Vision. Of course, if you did become a better writer and speller because of your journal, so much the better. If you avoid this very important part of Vision building, you're in essence asking your Vision to sprout wings, fly away, and take root somewhere else. You don't want to do that, do you?

Strengthen Your Vision With Positive Associations

Have you ever heard a song on the radio and immediately thought of someone, or something? The association may remind you of a former boyfriend or girlfriend. Maybe that was "your song." Even though you may not have even seen that person in years, the association is still there. What great power our minds have in this way. Since we know that positive associations occur, let's use them to our advantage. What better way to continue to give your True Vision a life of its own than to give it its own anthem? Select an upbeat song, one that will inspire you and bring your Vision to the forefront of your mind. You may even want to pick a few songs to give your Vision a more invigorating force. For several years after the first hit movie *Rocky* was released, it seemed that the only music that you heard when you watched a boxing match on television was that theme song, as fighters headed to the ring. They associated themselves with Rocky, the lovable pug that gave it all he had, and ended up a winner not because of overwhelming skill, but because of his dogged persistence. It's a wonderful story with a great theme song. Another great "anthem" is the theme song from *Chariots of Fire*. The academy award-winning film about long ago Olympic runners. Today there are many songs, too numerous to mention, that you can use as an anthem.

Your association doesn't necessarily have to be as close as professional boxers would be to the Rocky theme song. You could adapt any sort of upbeat tune from any style of music. It's totally up to you. I would only add that the music should be able to move you emotionally. As you think about your True Vision when listening to your music, pump it up in the theater of the mind. Take it as far as it will go. If it's your desire to lose weight then picture everyone complimenting you at a party and staring at you as you walk into the room as your theme song plays in the background.

You are the hero of this Vision building exercise so (as Rocky would say) go for it! Use whatever visual image you want to make this event inspirational and, more importantly, real. If you walk into a party visualize all of the people who are there one by one. Look directly into their eyes as they look in astonishment at the weight that you've lost and how good you now look. Visualize what you're wearing and with whom you are attending the party. I've used several songs to help build my Vision. The only criterion for choosing your song(s) is that it must fill you with enthusiasm regarding your True Vision.

The People Connection

Early during the development of my own True Vision I was watching a biography on television of Turner Communications founder Ted Turner. I happened to notice a placard that was hanging on his wall that read: "Lead follow or get out of the way." How true I thought. **The only people** that you'll meet on your way to success are those who will want to lead you with their own experience, those who want to fall in line behind you, and finally, those who get in the way with their negative comments or deliberate attempts at sabotage. If this is the case, then make sure that you begin your journey to fulfilling your True Vision by eliminating as much negativity from your life as possible. At the same time, surround yourself with people who can help you achieve your True Vision.

Protect Your True Vision From Attack

You are excited. This is because you now have a True Vision of yourself climbing that mountain, starting that business, getting that pay raise, building that relationship, or losing those pounds. The first thing you probably want to do is shout it from the rooftops. It's a natural feeling to want to tell everyone why you're so excited. You want to call all of your friends and relatives and let them in on your newfound confidence. But don't do it! Never display a work in progress. Look at all of the great artists. Do they rush out to display their paintings after the first brush stroke? Of course not. They wait until their painting is complete, and then they share it with the world. You should do the same thing.

I'm not saying that you can't share your True Vision with one or two trusted friends. Just make sure they're not rivals. If you developed a Vision for obtaining that promotion that every other person in your office covets and proceeded to tell them all about it, don't you think that at least one or two of them would try to sabotage your efforts? Envy is a powerful force. How would you react if someone attempted to deter you by telling you how hard it is and how you might not be qualified? Your newfound Vision may have nothing whatsoever to do with the people that you work with, but it is still a mistake to reveal your painting until the finishing touches have been placed. The simple reason, unfortunately, is a green-eyed monster called jealousy. "But all of my friends already have more and have done more than I have. Why would they be jealous of little old me?" Well, that's your perception of "little old you," not necessarily their view of the situation.

People sometimes act strangely when it comes to another's success. There's no question that some are happy for you. That's why I say share your Vision when in fact you have something concrete to share.

However, there are those people who will try to demean you when you attempt to improve your life. No one wants to be left behind when you stand out by starting your own business, or plan on getting that big career advancement. No one wants to be reminded, by contrast, how much of a rut his or her own life might be in. Unfortunately, there are people who are simply too fragile themselves to handle another person's success with grace. They will attempt to push you down to make themselves look better.

At some point, when the time is right, without showing a painting before it's complete, and without bragging, it will become obvious that you're attempting to accomplish something of great magnitude in your life. At this time there will be those who step up and, for whatever reason, attempt to swat you down. The worst thing to do is to give these people fodder by arguing with them. They must be avoided because if you give them your time and a willing ear, they will destroy your Vision without you even realizing it until it's over.

I've seen many a True Vision fall by the wayside because of a negative spouse who exerted something I call "pillow talk." Pillow talk is a relentless verbal bombardment that only spouses can administer because of the amount of time that is spent with them in all sorts of circumstances. Pillow talk can be positive or negative. When negative, it's only a short time before your Vision will be trashed. Negative pillow talk is like the ocean water washing in on the shoreline rocks. A few waves don't have much affect. But eventually, the onslaught of non-stop waves rolling in one after the other, day after day, week after week, month after month, does have a great effect! It's only a matter of time before the rocks become rounded, actually molded into a new form by mere water. It's also only a matter of time before a persistent negative spouse dismantles your Vision piece by piece.

"I can't avoid my spouse, my co-worker, my neighbor, or others I see daily and care about," you say. I am not claiming that you should. I certainly don't want you to be estranged from your spouse or any family member. So you have to set up "ground rules" when you're around those whom you are close to who do not yet believe in your True Vision.

With some family members you might try something like this: "You know what I'm in the middle of accomplishing [always speak in the positive] so I would appreciate it if you would not mention that particular subject when I'm around. If you do mention it I will be forced to leave. I don't want to leave so please let's talk about something else." Will this work with the most negative of friends and relatives? Maybe not; however, short of avoiding them this is your best strategy.

Obviously, with your spouse you'll have to handle yourself a little differently. I suggest pointing out all of the benefits that your True Vision will have for both of you once accomplished. If your Vision is to lose weight, make sure that you point out to your spouse, who may be feeling just a little insecure about your changing body, that you're doing it for him or her. You want to look more attractive, in part, for that person. Maybe you can even convince your spouse to adopt your Vision as his or her own, and the two of you can succeed together. There are few systems that work better than two people working in harmony toward the same True Vision, especially a husband and wife. You would be very lucky if your spouse showers you with positive pillow talk, which in turn will increase the intensity and focus of your True Vision. Sharing your True Vision with the right person at the proper time is always a good idea.

I made the mistake on a few occasions of allowing myself to be carried away by enthusiasm and bragging to some people that I was going to become a millionaire by my thirty-first birthday. One "friend," who was himself financially well off but still short of millionaire status, stated emphatically that it would never happen. He then threw at me a laundry list of reasons why it was impossible for me to become a millionaire. He spouted off with such vigor it was as if he was a prosecutor in a court of law arguing for the death penalty of my idea. My faint response of "You'll see" just didn't have the same fervor. He was not convinced and by the time I left his company that evening I wasn't so sure myself. Fortunately, I turned that episode around, and used it to create my next True Vision journal entry: "I not only have many positive reasons to achieve my Vision, I also have one negative reason. I'll show this big mouth who can do what!" Some might consider this to be a rash display of overconfidence, but you cannot allow your True Vision to be stolen by a negative force!

Never hesitate to use what is at hand to further grow your Vision. In short, I turned the situation around. I used the power of his negative force against him, something akin to mental jiu-jitsu for want of a better comparison. But what if I had several people like him spewing their negativity in my direction? Would it have cost me my True Vision? It certainly would have become more difficult, wouldn't it? There is only so much negative abuse that your psyche can handle before your fervor and your Vision start to fade, and futility takes over. Try to avoid these types by keeping your Vision to yourself. If this isn't possible at least give the people around you ground rules when you're together.

People Who Can Help

Let's turn to a more positive topic: those individuals who can help you grow your Vision. I only realized years later when I looked back, but my own particular Vision took root in a pumpkin patch just prior to my ninth birthday. One day when I was harassing my father (Sam) for a new bicycle, he proposed an idea that as he put it, "would give you all the extra spending money a kid your age would ever want." Since Dad always kept a very sizeable vegetable garden and he didn't quite trust me as the solo pilot of the riding lawn mower, I had a feeling I knew where this was headed. "We'll plant a nice big pumpkin patch, and you can take care of them. When it comes time, you can sell them by the side of the road and whatever you make is yours." A great plan, I thought, except of course for the part where I had to "take care of them." Oh, and the part where I was going to have to "sell them" was a little intimidating as well to a kid my age, I remember thinking. "What the heck, let's do it," I replied, full of childish bravado.

That summer and fall my career as an entrepreneur was launched. Up to that point in my life I had never worked so hard. Nothing even came close to the weed pulling marathon sessions that I somehow made it through on those sizzling hot summer days. Every time I yanked a weed from its roots there was another one in front of it. Sweat poured from my small brow like water from a fountain. "Nope, there is no end in sight," I remarked under my breath one particularly hot and dreary day. "I'll be here picking weeds with my face to the dirt until I'm a teenager, or even older," I remember muttering, even though my father was always in that pumpkin patch by my side helping. It seemed like I weeded the garden just about every day although it was probably more like once a week. I remember how black my hands were after each trip to the garden. I'd hold my hands up so that my father could see my palms, and say, "Look." "That's okay," he'd reply, "That means that you've been working hard." I learned at an early age that getting my hands dirty from hard work was nothing to be ashamed of.

Suddenly one day my father told me that it was time to "harvest the pumpkin crop." I had no idea what that meant, but I knew it had to be better than weeding. I blurted out, "Does that mean we're finished with all of this stinking weeding?" He gave me a stern look and I feigned a brief smile in return, "Not that I mind it that much, you know." "Time to sell the pumpkins!" Dad exclaimed. Finally, the last weed was pulled. When it came time to sell them I remember vividly attempting to pick up pumpkins that seemed almost as large as I was. Of course, I didn't mind because those were the One Dollar size!

Each day after school, and all day on weekends, I was in business. My father would hitch the tractor up to the big trailer that was full of pumpkins and bring them out front by the roadside. Together we would unload them and make sure each one was properly displayed and marked. I can still remember the feeling of success as I stood on a chair looking out of the kitchen window and seeing a car pull up to examine our crop. I would happily go out and greet my potential customers. Whether they bought one or not, selling was a heck of a lot better than weeding I thought. However, buy them they did! My cash drawer was one of my grandfather's old cigar boxes, and I kept every cent in that box. My mother (Ella) taught me how to make change that fall. I also learned how to greet customers, display my product, and keep somewhat of an inventory. By the end of the pumpkin season, which is the day after Thanksgiving, I'd made over five hundred dollars. This was a fortune to a nine-year-old.

True to his word my father allowed me to keep every dollar. However, my mother stepped in and brought up a new subject. It seems that such sizeable fortunes were meant to be kept in something called a bank. I didn't know much about banks. What I did know was that they kept your money for you, and that meant I couldn't get to it, so I immediately took a disliking to banks. (My feelings toward them didn't improve over twenty years later when I was forced to go to 33 banks in order to get a business loan.) After a lengthy debate (my mother talked while I listened while issuing a mild protest now and again), it was decided. I would keep ten percent to spend on a bike, or on any other item I wanted, and would put the rest in my very own bank account. I could use the bank money for birthday and Christmas presents for family and friends, and for other worthy causes. Also, if there were something that I really wanted I could make a withdrawal now and then. That seemed reasonable. What didn't seem as fair was the other thing they told me I was saving for. Something in the far distant future, so many years away that I thought it would never get here. It was called college.

Good Friends And Loved Ones Help Fuel The Vision

The pumpkin experience was a great one to have at such an early age. It taught me so many important lessons, not the least of which is that hard work, directed in a proper manner, is rewarded. To those of you who haven't had similar experiences it is never too late to go out and get them. Just remember to surround yourself with people who will either help you, or fall in behind you, in your quest to build your own True Vision!

My True Vision continued to blossom as I grew into my teens. I had a friend who inadvertently helped throw more logs on the fire of my Vision very early on. We would go for long walks and talk about how we were going to shake the business world by its trunk. We would see various businesses and explain to each other how we would make them better. "That tire store should add another bay to their building. Look at the long line," I would say. "Oh yeah," my friend would add, "they're probably losing over two hundred dollars per hour the way they're doing it now." In reality we were busy solving problems that didn't exist for businesses that were quite successful and didn't need a couple of kids critiquing them. However, while I didn't know it then, these types of conversations furthered my own True Vision of becoming successful in business.

I'm very fortunate indeed. I have a wife, Peggy, who remains my greatest supporter, and I am hers. It was like this from the start. I shared my True Vision with her very early when we were dating, and she became an instant believer, and, I want to stress, my only one at the time. I remember many evenings where we didn't have enough money to go out on a real date, and we would just sit and talk. She would let me talk on endlessly about my Vision, interrupting only to ask a question, add to the picture, or come up with ideas I'd never thought of. I can state without hesitation that without her by my side it would have been much more difficult to realize my True Vision, and in fact, I might have failed. Everyone needs a sounding board, but of course she was far more than that to me. She was then, and to this day remains, my best friend, and the love of my life.

Hopefully, there is someone in your life whom you can trust and who can add a fresh perspective that will assist you in turning your True Vision into a reality. Is your spouse like this? I hope so. Your spouse may be a late bloomer who will come along after he or she sees a little success. Remember you're not looking for a business partner. You're just looking for someone who is like-minded, one or more people who have either been where you're going or are generally supportive of your Vision in other ways. Maybe all they do is listen while you describe your Vision. Fine, you'll take it. If you're fortunate enough to find someone with a like mind who supports you too, then you are far ahead of the crowd.

Is your True Vision to become an entrepreneur? Join an entrepreneurs club, or make positive associations with other entrepreneurs in some other way. Are you looking for that big promotion? Then join a local business club, and mingle with people who can further your career and help feed your executive Vision. Always be mindful of your associations because we tend to take on the traits of those with whom we spend the most time. Make sure that you're absorbing the proper qualities and are spending most of your time with others who have a positive direction in their own lives. It's often not deliberate, and sometimes completely unconscious, that we take on mannerisms and character traits of those who occupy our time. Let's keep all of our associations positive and this will help keep the Vision growing. Let's now take a closer look at "Vision Steps," which are essential qualities that are needed to move your True Vision into a reality!

chapter four

VISION STEP:
POSITIVE SELF-DISCIPLINE

The first and best victory is to conquer self.
— Plato

Have you created a positive, long-lasting, red-hot True Vision? Is your Vision constantly being fueled by the various techniques we've been discussing, and by positive relationships, all recorded in your journal? I am convinced that the biggest reason for failure in any major endeavor is the absence or weakness of an enduring True Vision. If you truly already see your True Vision as a reality then the next several Vision Steps can actually be fun.

I know you realize that if you truly want to achieve something above and beyond what most people accomplish, it will take effort above and beyond what most people display. **It's simple logic: in most cases you get out of something what you put into it. When there's little effort put forth there's little benefit received.**

Once your True Vision is firmly established it's time to make it into a reality—and it's here where some complain a little. "Self-discipline" you say? "Um, no thanks." In fact, it's not as hard as you might think. If you have done your Vision homework, it can even be fun. I admit you don't hear the word "self-discipline" used much anymore. It's almost as if you're reaching back into the dark ages and dredging up some sort of medieval torture device by the name of discipline, like the rack or the ball and chain.

When some first hear the word "self-discipline" they recoil, not feeling confident about traveling down that road. Well, relax. When you have a powerful True Vision and see the results in your mind's eye, you're far more willing to put forth the amount of time and effort needed to turn that Vision into a reality. And when that's the case, self-discipline can even boost your self-confidence! In fact, that's the reason that I refer to it as "Positive Self-Discipline." Let's look at those words differently from this point forward. I truly believe that you will enjoy exercising your Positive Self-Discipline knowing that each time you do, you move that much closer to what you really want in life.

My favorite definition of the words Positive Self-Discipline: "to gain control through obedience and training." So, who needs this? We all do. We live in a time when virtually every temptation known to the modern world is laid before our feet. While this makes life easy, more fun and comfortable, it's not always productive or healthy. In fact, the more opportunity that you have to be extravagant in your life, the more Positive Self-Discipline you need!

The American Medical Association reports that just over six out of ten Americans are overweight—that is over sixty percent of our population; why? Simply put, because they can. Never before in the history of the world has there been more of an opportunity to indulge in the excesses of life, whether it is food, cigarettes, alcohol, or just spending too much money. In its wake extravagance has left a litany of unnecessary pain: obesity, divorce, substance addiction, depression, bankruptcy, and more. I believe that every problem has a root, a place where it started, a seed that was planted, took hold and grew. At the root of many of today's maladies is a lack of self-discipline. Those afflicted have not yet learned how to truly gain control through personal obedience to what is helpful, healthful behavior in every aspect of their lives. This seems harsh to some because they cannot see beyond any immediate sacrifice to the ultimate fulfillment of their True Vision. However, I am sure that you understand why this is so important. You are interested in the achievement of your True Vision and know now that this takes working smart and a little sacrifice.

I know this firsthand. I received a good overview of our society when I employed more than one thousand people in sixteen states in my first sizeable business. I am certain, as any of my former key employees will agree, that as the number of personal problems goes up, the chance for career success and success in other key areas of one's life goes down. There is a direct cause and effect relationship between these areas of your life. The tension and mental stress that some people place on themselves through overindulgence and a lack of Positive Self-Discipline are frightening. Of course, you can't focus on your career when you are cheating on your spouse. Naturally, you have a difficult time getting up for work in the morning if you're out late at night drinking to excess. You have only so much energy, and if you choose to use that energy in ways that are personally destructive, naturally you will pay a price, as you have less of it available for your family and career. It is time to drop the excuses and concentrate on what is important and positive in life and take full ownership of your successes as well as your failures!

For example, let's take the person who battles a weight problem. It is difficult to lose weight when there are all of those enablers around you telling you that it's not your fault, it's simply in your genes. After all, your parents were heavy. Now, this may be true. You may have a harder time losing weight than some other people, and some other people may have a more difficult time losing weight than you. My question is this: what are you going to do about your weight problem? Will you worry about the fact that your genes do not allow you to lose weight as quickly as someone else? That seems like a waste of time to me. And it won't help solve your problem either. All it does is give you a Shield of Excuse so that you can feel better about failing!

Do You Use The Shield Of Excuse?

Let's start by gaining control using Positive Self-Discipline and put it to use on a daily basis. First, you need to do the one thing that places self-discipline truly with the self. You need to admit that you are totally responsible for what happens to you and to let go of the Shield of Excuse. The Shield of Excuse is a huge imaginary iron shield, one that is easy to put in front of you but once in place difficult to remove. It protects us head to toe from all of the bad feelings that we might get when someone tries to attach blame to us for an action for which we are in fact responsible. It is a convenient mechanism that temporarily protects the psyche. Unfortunately, using the Shield of Excuse also prevents us from taking responsibility and learning from our mistakes so that we can have the sort of life we desire. **The truth is you will not live the life you were meant to live and realize your True Vision if**

you are using the Shield of Excuse. This will ultimately prevent you from improving in key areas, increasing the possibility of success, and thus increasing your reward.

You may remember the lady who sued McDonald's corporation because they served her a cup of coffee that was too hot. There are people who have also sued McDonald's for causing their weight gain. Other lawsuits claim everything from a department store's air conditioning being too cold and causing a customer to catch a cold to a waitress being so rude that the customer had nightmares. When does it all stop? I believe it ends when each individual removes the Shield of Excuse from himself, and begins to take full responsibility for his own actions. Many people blame trial lawyers for these types of suits, but keep in mind that the most aggressive trial lawyer only goes to work after *you* hire him. The decision to begin is always going to be yours first. You must be willing to consider making a fresh start. Reach out and embrace your Vision for a positive change in your life. Leave the Shield of Excuse behind and take full responsibility for your own actions!

Ultimately You Get What You Deserve

You are totally responsible for what happens to you in most every case. What about the man who was run over by a bus? He didn't deserve to die, you say. Maybe not, but perhaps he didn't look both ways prior to crossing the street. Whatever sort of life that the man lived, good or bad, in that one instant because he neglected to look both ways, he received exactly what he deserved. Your uncle died of cancer. He didn't deserve that. Then again, he did smoke three packs of cigarettes a day, so in a sense he did deserve it.

My point is that, more or less, you have deserved virtually everything that has happened to you so far in your lifetime. Furthermore, you will deserve just about everything that happens to you during the remainder of your life. I'm using the word "deserve" as one being worthy of what he or she has attained, the final result of the accumulation of one's actions. I am not trying to use the word "deserve" as a stick to beat you over the head, although it may feel that way. You are in essence currently living with the end result of all of your actions or lack of actions up to this point in your life. If you're not satisfied with this end result the good part is that you can change it going forward. You can be the person that you have always wanted to be, starting today. Visualize yourself at that point in the future where you are indeed satisfied with what you have become. Attaining your True Vision begins today and reaches out to reward you time and again right up to the end of your life. However, this will only happen if you drop the Shield of Excuse and take responsibility for all your actions. Can you do this? Ask yourself: Are you mature enough to step forward and take responsibility for the rest of your life?

Let's acknowledge that some people get what they seem not to deserve, and others never seem to get what they do deserve. How many of us have heard about the man who died at the age of ninety-seven and smoked all of his life and the young man who tragically died of lung cancer and never smoked? However, I am not writing about life's unfairness, or good genetics versus bad, and I'm not writing about exceptions to the rule. I am writing about the rule. Don't attempt to legitimize your case by creating exceptions. If you use these exceptions to the rule to defend your current three packs a day habit, or eating foods that you know are not healthy, you are using the Shield of Excuse. This particular shield is called "the exception to the rule shield." It goes something like this, "I had a friend whose uncle lived to be 95 and he smoked every day of his life." All sorts of shields are used frequently.

Any of these sound familiar?

- It's not my fault that I have a slow metabolism
- How am I supposed to exercise when it's raining?
- It's only one piece of cake and after all, everyone else is eating it.
- I know I can't afford it; I'll just use my credit card again.
- How am I supposed to work a full-time job and develop a business too?
- You can't expect me to sit there and not have a beer when everyone else is drinking.
- It was a harmless affair. She/he meant nothing to me.
- I've smoked all my life, how can I quit now?
- How can I exercise when I have to work late?
- If it were not for office politics I would have had that promotion.

Why is it so important for you to accept the blame for your actions? Because as soon as you use the Shield of Excuse and put it firmly in front of you no one else can remove it! It's even hard for you to remove it after a while, and why not, as it protects you and makes you feel better. The minute you reach for that shield you stop trying. Part of us truly does give up when we use the Shield of Excuse. If you use the "I can't lose weight because I have poor genes" shield I know that the battle is lost before it is even begun. You can never stop smoking when you use the "I have smoked for twenty years and can't stop now" shield. And who ever heard of a successful entrepreneur who used the "I can never succeed in this lousy economy" shield? At least the successful ones don't think that way. Successful people, those with a True Vision for their lives, step up and take responsibility!

The only way to long-term success in any undertaking is to drop the Shield of Excuse and to continue to move forward. You have to begin today to release your reliance on whichever shield is holding you back. It may be difficult at first but it's worth it. I want you to fully own all of your actions. The only way to do that is to understand that you really are responsible for virtually everything that happens to you. The time to remove the Shield of Excuse is now! The reward is a better life in every way. When you can get to this point Positive Self-Discipline becomes automatic. In fact, it gets to be a way of life that is very rewarding. However, let's not get ahead of ourselves. Now that you realize who is responsible for you, let's move on to specific examples of people using Self-Discipline to get what they want in life and how you can too.

Positive Self-Discipline Becomes A Lifestyle

When I started my first successful company I was so busy that I noticed I was not making time for many things that were beneficial to me. One of those things was my regularly scheduled almost daily workout. At the time I was quick to use the Shield of Excuse to avoid taking responsibility for skipping these rejuvenating exercise sessions. I used the "no time for that activity" shield. This helped rationalize the fact that I was not planning my day very well. It made me feel much better about skipping my usual workouts. In December of that same year I came down with the worst case of the flu that I'd ever gotten. In fact, until that point I had not been sick all that much as an adult. Was there a direct correlation between skipping my workouts and getting sick? It has been well documented that exercise does in fact enhance the immune system. I knew from past experience that when I was in top shape I didn't seem to get sick and if I did, it would only last a couple of days. When I realized what was happening I made sure not to skip my workouts.

I remember arriving home one evening around eight o'clock and heading right off to the gym. I didn't do this to be an exercise martyr or some sort of health fanatic. I did this because I know how easy it is to let it go and to fall into an unhealthy lifestyle. I could have easily used the "it's too late tonight shield" to get out of my workout. Instead I used Positive Self-Discipline to form a schedule that was ultimately good for me. This was not as hard to do as you might imagine because I had formed a Vision of myself as an "athletic businessman." I pictured in the theater of my mind exactly how I wanted to look and feel. I knew what I had to do to achieve it, and that was to exercise no less than six days per week. Could I have used the "it's too late tonight" shield that evening? Yes, but I also knew that the week was not going to get less hectic. What I didn't need was to start off the week behind on accomplishing my fitness Vision. Instead, I exercised Positive Self-Discipline to assist me in fulfilling what I consider a very important True Vision. (Little did I realize at the time that the consistency and intensity for my regular workouts would lead me twenty years later to being recognized by GUINNESS WORLD RECORDS three times!)

What I came to discover was that it became much easier to devote time to exercise. It didn't become easier because my schedule became less complicated, but because my Positive Self-Discipline became stronger. When you finish your workout and realize that you did it, you feel great. In addition, you never again want the feeling that you let yourself down by missing out on that great feeling. **By meeting your obligations you are not just telling yourself, but <u>proving</u> to yourself, that you are for real and nothing will stand in your way.** Your plans mean something and are not to be discarded because of a time problem, or for any other reason!

When you do things like this it tells you a lot about yourself. You become a strong believer in what you can do, and that's when your True Vision really takes on a life of its own. In other words, when you start building Positive Self-Discipline, you build mental toughness. This is even more important than physical toughness in terms of fulfilling your True Vision. The power of Positive Self-Discipline is able to spread across many boundaries. I found that I became more efficient within my business day as well. I was better able to dictate the pace of my day, instead of having it dictate to me. It didn't take long for Positive Self-

Discipline to become a way of life. I didn't walk around thinking about it; it just became part of me. I didn't need much forethought or even a feeling of having to agonize over it as I did when I first began. I would sometimes hear people say, how can you stick to such a schedule? When in fact I was thinking, how can you not? By discarding the Shield of Excuse you will set yourself up for achieving the kind of Positive Self-Discipline that will ultimately lead you to realizing your True Vision!

What is your True Vision? If you're trying to lose weight, and you and your doctor decide on an exercise plan, stick to it! If it involves getting up each morning at 6 a.m. to exercise, then drop the Shield of Excuse and do it! If it seemed a good time of the day to exercise when you planned it then it probably is a good time. Don't allow the early morning hour to color your judgment so that you begin your day surrendering your Positive Self-Discipline to short-term emotion. It's the short-term emotion that helps create the Shield of Excuse that will ultimately prevent you from fulfilling your True Vision. The short-term emotion cries out to you don't do it! Go back to bed: it's too early, I'm tired, and it's raining outdoors. Don't use the weather Shield of Excuse. Understand that if your exercise plan relies on jogging outdoors then there will be those cold and rainy days. Don't use the, "I'm too tired" shield either. Get up and exercise on less sleep than you're used to. You will see two things happen: The first is that you'll sleep well that evening. The second is that you'll think twice before staying up late the night before a scheduled morning workout. What's wrong with that?

The Positive Self-Discipline Of A Champion

I had the privilege of working with one of the greatest heavyweight boxing champions in the history of the sport, Joe Frazier. Even if you're not a fan of the "sweet science" you have undoubtedly heard of the three great fights that Joe Frazier and Muhammed Ali had back in the 1970s. During their most memorable fight Joe Frazier knocked down Muhammed Ali in the final round. Up to that point Muhammed Ali had never been knocked off his feet in a professional bout. Joe Frazier was truly one of the greatest!

I hired Joe Frasier to do a series of television commercials and to be a spokesperson for my company. During the time that we spent together I discovered why Joe Frazier had become the champion that he was destined to be. His work habits were second to none. He would arrive early on the set knowing all of his lines and do countless takes until the director agreed that he had gotten exactly what he wanted. Whether it be shooting commercials or greeting the hundreds of fans that came out to see him at our store promotions, Joe was tireless in his efforts day after day. He was always the epitome of professionalism, poise and dignity. I just had to find out what propelled this man to the very heights in perhaps the toughest professional sport.

When I asked Joe about how he got to be heavyweight boxing champion of the world, he spoke intently of Vision and discipline along with other Vision Steps that helped drive him to the very top of his profession and kept him there for many years. He described to me his regular daily routine. He would arise just before dawn and do five miles of roadwork. When he was finished with his run he would then go to the gym to do calisthenics, hit the speed bag for several minutes, and then do many rounds on the heavy bag. On certain days he would also spar five or more rounds with various young eager sparring partners. Only after all of this was completed would he go eat breakfast. And most days he would go back to the gym for a second workout! When I asked him how he found the Positive Self-Discipline to perform this schedule day after grueling day, he looked at me intently and said, "Because I could see myself as champion and I knew what it would take to get there." This is a testimony to the power of Positive Self-Discipline planted firmly on the base of a supreme True Vision! Joe Frazier became Heavyweight Champion of the World. You too can also reach the height of your chosen field, or accomplish anything else that you desire, as long as you begin with True Vision and carry it forth with the following Vision Steps, the first being Positive Self-Discipline.

Start With Small Victories

In the development of any skill or ability you don't start out as a master. Joe Frazier didn't begin his journey by performing strenuous workouts every day, by fighting his first bout for the heavyweight title. He started with small victories, carefully building the Vision. It's important to remind ourselves that becoming really good at Positive Self-Discipline takes a little time and effort. Take it step by step. I like the feeling of small victories because what you can accomplish on a small scale you can also eventually accomplish on a large scale in time. For example, if you want to start a business but don't have an idea, practice exercising some Positive Self-Discipline by brainstorming at least two potential ideas each week. The ideas don't have to be your first choice for a business just as long as you think that they're viable ones as a result of research. At the end of a few weeks you may have several ideas that you've researched with which to make your final decision. More importantly, you'll also have several more weeks of practicing Positive Self-Discipline. The mere act of setting time aside for five straight days will help you begin to develop Positive Self-Discipline. It can also be the beginning of a lucrative business that will bring you all of the money and independence that you have ever wanted!

Creating such small victories helps build your confidence. We eat one bite at a time and it's the same with our Vision. Many times I've gotten involved with people attempting to lose weight only to hear them say that they wanted to lose five pounds a week. My first question to them was always, "Did you put the weight on at the rate of five pounds a week?" The answer of course was always no. Some people are looking for a fast, easy way to accomplish their True Vision. If they can't have easy they will at least take fast. Unfortunately, it doesn't work that way with weight loss, or with any other worthwhile endeavor. It takes lots of small victories sometimes to accomplish one large victory. Some people may have practiced wrong behaviors over and over again until they were so ingrained in their mind that they became second nature, and now they actually seem right. This can all be undone, but it's best to take it in small steps in order to avoid that burned-out feeling that happens just before you fail.

If you achieve one small victory at a time, you'll be taking the proper corrective action to solve the problem. You could begin by avoiding that dessert that you normally eat on weekends. Are you overeating to compensate for something that you really want, but don't think you can achieve? Are you overusing food as a reward to encourage yourself in other areas? Do you overeat to compensate for certain stressful situations in your life? Do you overeat because that's the type of environment that you grew up in? Maybe you grew up with a lack of food and that's the reason you're now overeating. Each person has his or her own reason for continuing a negative behavior. But, while it's good to become aware of why you are overeating, the reason is not nearly as important as what you are going to do about it today, right now! Practice the Positive Self-Discipline to meet your problem head on. Sure, you could fail, but if you think about it you're already failing by not trying! As a wise baseball coach once told me, "You will not hit 100% of the balls that you do not swing at." It's the same with every attempt at whatever Vision you are trying to achieve.

By achieving small victories you'll begin a pattern of success through Positive Self-Discipline that will take you anywhere that you want to go. You must first begin the process by attempting something that you know you can do. When you succeed at it you are proving to yourself that Positive Self-Discipline works. After you become a believer in the power that you have to effect real change in your life, you will no longer be controlled by your weakest emotion, but rather by your most inspiring True Vision!

chapter five

VISION STEP:
CREATING WINNING HABITS

Bad Habits just seem to find us.
Good habits must be found by us.
   —Bob Natoli

Once we've acted with Positive Self-discipline we've traveled farther down the road toward realizing our Vision. And when we achieve Positive Self-Discipline a most powerful ally begins to act on our behalf, habit!

We are all creatures of habit. You don't think so? Just move your wastebasket from one side of the room to another. The next time that you crumple up a piece of paper to toss away you'll be throwing to a spot on the floor where the wastebasket used to sit. Still not convinced that you're a slave to habit? Just try removing your watch for the day. When you want to know what time it is you will be staring straight into your bare wrist. What route do you take to work each day? Where do you sit if you attend religious services? Where do you sit at the dinner table? What aisle do you walk down when you begin grocery shopping? What are the brands that you purchase over and over again? Getting my point? This has nothing to do with intelligence. It's merely that automatic pilot called habit taking over.

Creating Winning Habits is an essential Vision Step on the path to achieving your True Vision. In fact, every victory in your life, as well as every defeat, has been shaped by habit. It has been your bad habits that have caused you to fail so far in whatever endeavor you've been trying to achieve. As Habit, that most powerful automatic pilot precedes every great accomplishment, as well as every resounding defeat.

I once saw a middle-aged man in a hospital bed hooked up to a respirator, drawing shallow breaths as he attempted to get more air into his lungs. This was a pretty sad sight. What was even more pitiful was that in his right hand was an unlit cigarette! While the hospital of course would never have allowed him to smoke that cigarette, he must have felt comforted by its very presence. It's obvious what habit preceded that monumental failure. Conversely, when you see an extremely fit person walk past you on the street, you can be sure of exactly what Winning Habit has preceded this particular look.

The truth is, if you don't consciously build good Winning Habits, you will unconsciously build bad ones. The person who spent a lifetime smoking was, at the outset, obviously not consciously focused on the end result of his behavior. If he had been, he might have chosen another path. One day that smoker decided to join his friends and light up. This is how that particular bad habit usually starts. He only smoked that one cigarette the first day and it might not have tasted all that good. Soon enough, however, after spending more time with his friends, he was smoking two a day and then three. Before long he was smoking a pack a day. Some people, as you know, far exceed even that. Heavy smokers are said to smoke almost four cigarettes an hour or one cigarette every sixteen minutes! Now that is a habit worth breaking!

This negative habit began unconsciously by smoking that first cigarette. This person did not have a conscious smoke free habit planned for his life so the void of not having a Winning Habit left a place open for the unconscious bad habit of smoking to begin—the act of smoking that first cigarette. We have about sixteen waking hours in a day. Those sixteen hours will be filled with some sort of activity, good or bad. You have to consciously choose to fill them with Winning Habits and, if not, they'll be filled with negative habits. In other words, your time will be filled with something one way or the other. Build Winning Habits, as they will last a lifetime and help you achieve your True Vision.

Let's not forget about that other person we talked about, the guy on the street who was obviously well muscled and lean. No question, he's quite conscious of the end result of his Winning Habit of regular exercise. He has successfully cultivated that Winning Habit, which is bearing obvious results, a fit body. Unlike the smoker who fell unconsciously into his habit, the person who begins and maintains the exercise habit must first consciously begin this Winning Habit-forming behavior. He showed up at the gym one day and began to create a habit that will yield benefits in every aspect of his life. Whether this first exercise session was enjoyable or not is unimportant. The important thing is that over time not only will it become enjoyable, but beneficial as well.

Once again, I emphasize, if you don't create your own Winning Habits you will fall into one that is not so positive. Bad habits just seem to find us. Good ones need to be found by us. They then need to be worked on a little each day. Either way you will be changed, for better or for worse. You'll be able to either thank or curse the habit that got you there. Make no mistake about it, whether you are cruising to victory or sliding toward defeat, habit will be the final stop just prior to arriving.

Anything Which Can Be Learned Can Be Unlearned

The bad news is that a bad habit is rarely just dropped. The good news is that a bad habit can be replaced with a Winning Habit. According to a recent study reported in the *European Journal of Social Psychology*, it takes an average of 66 days to create a habit. This cutting edge research is the first to take a close look at how long it actually takes to create a Winning Habit in your life. The researchers investigated how long it took to cause repetition of certain behaviors to get to a stage where they became automatic. Prior to this study most people believed that it took only 21 days to form a positive habit. While 21 days is a very good start, and with some behaviors may be long enough to do the trick, 66 days is the average number it takes to make an action automatic enough to become a habit (a more difficult habit could take longer). This means that you must exercise Positive Self-Discipline for about 66 days in order to replace that bad habit. By that time a new Winning Habit can be formed.

One of the reasons that you can't stop smoking is that you've learned to associate the negative act of smoking with many positive places and pleasurable things. If you list the three places where you smoke the most what you'll find is that you have created, unconsciously of course, some very positive associative habits regarding where and when you smoke. For example, a cigarette after a delicious dinner—there's nothing like it, right? That first cigarette with your morning coffee tastes great, doesn't it? That cigarette that you puff on the way to work while listening to your favorite radio station tastes great too. Going out for the evening? Don't forget your cigarettes. A good time and a cigarette seem to go together, don't they? The same can be said for most habits.

Negative things seem to attach themselves to other more positive things and this gives them even more power to control your life. The same can be said for a doughnut and a cup of coffee. Could you have a small cookie and a cup of coffee? "Sure, but it just wouldn't be the same," you say. Well, not at first it wouldn't. The same can be said for the person who is neck high in debt. This person has learned through positive associations, such as the pleasure of buying a gift for a family member or good friend on the spur of the moment, that a credit card is a good thing. A vacation, a new car, the list is endless. The immediate gratification seems to outweigh the ultimate financial downfall that is sure to follow. The evils of abuse are not being judged because the positive immediate association is so pleasing.

Bad habits are not easily dropped when practiced over time. However, it's easier than you think to replace bad habits with good ones. Instead of having a cigarette after your evening meal, for instance, replace it with a ten or fifteen minute walk. If you're married, take your spouse along with you. If you have children, take them too. I understand that this does not resolve your possible addiction to nicotine. If your addiction to nicotine is so great, then see your doctor and ask about a temporary nicotine substitute. Just make sure that you're replacing the habit of having a cigarette with a Winning Habit such as walking. This will put the power back in your hands and also create a new habit, which will extend your life instead of shortening it. Soon you will not want to miss your daily walk as that will become a Winning Habit.

Begin to break a negative habit by breaking the negative relationships that support and enable that habit. If you have a good friend who tends to smoke around you, politely ask that person to stop. You may end up leading that person away from a self-destructive habit too. On the other hand, if they can't do that much for you, how good a friend is she?

When you think about replacing your negative habit with a positive one, remember that anything which is learned can be unlearned.

Here is where you'll need to exercise Positive Self-Discipline at least in the beginning. Once the new Winning Habit is formed the Positive Self-Discipline you will need to draw on will be far less and eventually not needed at all. It will be your new improved Winning Habit-forming behavior that will take over and once again you will be on automatic pilot. Only this time you'll be headed in the right direction. The key is to tell yourself that you're going to perform the Winning Habit for just 66 days. Committing yourself for 66 days is much easier than setting out on a different course for a lifetime, isn't it? At the end of 66 days you'll most likely find that you've created a new Winning Habit, one that can help you achieve your True Vision.

Have You Ever Taken A Short-Term Gain For A Long-Term Loss?

Have you ever taken a short-term gain for a long-term loss? I bet if you have a bad habit that's exactly what you're doing just about every day.

I know you realize that if you want to achieve your True Vision it will take effort above and beyond what most people are willing to put forth. It's simple logic but it bears repeating: in most cases you get out of something what you put into it. When there's little effort put forth there's little benefit received. Some people have a difficult time understanding this and want their reward immediately. They may not realize it, but they're taking a short-term gain for a long-term loss. They want to feel good *now* regardless of the long-term consequences.

For example: you'd love to lose thirty pounds, but what do you say to the person who offers you a jelly doughnut? Is it something like, "What does one doughnut matter? I'm not going to start my diet until the first of the month anyway. Everyone is enjoying the doughnuts so why can't I?" Whether you know it or not, you not only failed to exercise Positive Self-discipline, but you've just used the Shield of Excuse to rationalize a short-term gain (eating the jelly doughnut) for a long-term loss (continuing to gain weight). But some people seem unable to take the long-term view when it comes to making themselves feel better. They're not necessarily worried about what might happen years or even months from now. They don't want to deny themselves something that will make them feel better now and so the cycle of the negative habit continues. In order to fulfill your True Vision, however, you need to reframe your thought pattern. You need to take a short-term loss (skipping the doughnut) for a long-term gain (a healthier, better looking body).

Let's look at another example, a man cheating on his spouse. I'm quite sure that the man is not purposely trying to become estranged from his children or his wife. No, a good parent doesn't want to be separated from his family. What he is thinking about is enjoying the moment, the immediate pleasure that he'll get from his affair. He's taking a short-term gain (intimacy with an attractive woman), which in this case leads to a long-term loss (the estrangement of his wife and children). **I've heard men bravely state, "I would die for my family." No doubt they would. My question to them would be this; Are you brave enough to "live" for your family?** Living for your family means taking many short-term losses for the ultimate long-term gain, a long and satisfying relationship with your spouse and children, which will lead to a happier life in the long-term. Ask yourself, is the short-term gain worth the long-term loss?

This type of bravery may not be the same adrenaline-pumping heroism we feel when we think about how we would stand and fight for our loved ones against a horde of thugs, robbers and murderers. Rather, living for your family is about making the right choices on a daily basis (some of them very mundane), but all of them with the long-term perspective in mind. Turning away from the short-term gain at the cost of a long-term loss is difficult, especially when you find yourself in a position where you're tempted. Isn't it better to avoid something that can cause pain to you and to those whom you love the most, right from the beginning?

If you're going to achieve your True Vision you need to master the art of *deferred gratification*. Taking the short-term loss for the long-term gain is essential. What is your True Vision? There are plenty of examples below, which may speak directly to your own circumstances.

Bad Habit	Short-term Gain	Long-term Loss
Overeating.	Food is an age old comforter. Many positive memories are associated with food.	Weight gain. Self disappointment. Poor health.
Smoking.	Calming effect. Very pleasurable.	Cancer. Heart disease. Shortened life span.
Overuse of credit cards.	Convenient. Fast & easy.	Stress from the mounting bills. Potential bankruptcy if carried to extremes.
Lack of exercise on a regular basis.	Never inconvenienced. Never have to worry about fitting it into a schedule.	Never gets the positive effects of exercise: lower blood pressure and cholesterol, firmer fitter body, higher self-esteem, more energy.
Putting off a positive career advancement, such as starting your own business.	Safe feeling of staying well within your comfort zone.	Regrets later in life. Never following your true desire.
Alcohol or drug abuse.	Eases temporary emotional or physical pain. Aids in escapism.	Both physically and socially damaging!
Chronic gambling.	Occasional wins cause exhilaration.	Ultimate financial devastation.

Do any of the above apply to you? Maybe I didn't touch on the bad habit that's holding you back by giving you a short-term gain for a long-term loss. If I didn't, why don't you write it out right now? Set the book down and write out the bad habit that gives you that short-term gain. Write the exact short-term gain that you achieve from this bad habit and then next to it write the long-term loss that will inevitably come if you don't do something about it today!

While it's important to live in the moment and enjoy life's pleasures you have to be careful not to take a long-term loss for a short-term gain, especially when it directly impacts your True Vision. It doesn't matter how long you've had the particular habit you're trying to break. Anything that is learned can be unlearned, and a bad habit can keep you from achieving your True Vision.

We've already discussed that replacing a bad habit with a good one will help end that negative reign of terror in your life. This will stop the long-term loss that will eventually pull you down. We also know that it takes on average only 66 days to make or break most habits. Now, we'll consider other strategies that can help you to reverse your bad habit. Let's always be shooting for the long-term gain!

Affirmation Reminders

This next powerful tool is called affirmation reminders. The word affirmation means to assert positively. I believe that affirmations must be used properly and in conjunction with the right amount of action. When used as reminders they keep us on the right track in achieving our True Vision. That is because if I'm going to free myself of any bad habit, then I need to have a constant reminder. **Many times we fail not because we don't know how to succeed, but because the proper behavior is not first and foremost in our minds. In other words, we simply forget about the habit we're trying to break because of the many other things we have to deal with in our lives.** Writing an Affirmation Reminder on a card or slip of paper and placing it where we are able to see it acts as an instantaneous reminder of exactly what we are trying to accomplish.

Some time ago I helped a young woman named Kate with a weight problem. Kate lost thirty-five pounds in just less than six months. Happily, she has also managed to keep it off. But in the beginning, her progress was bumpy. Kate's biggest problem was not being able to keep the long-term devastating effects of overeating in the forefront of her mind.

She would make wonderful progress during the week, but found herself unable to stay away from harmful foods during the weekend. Do you have that problem too? Between Friday night and Monday morning she would invariably gain back the weight that she'd lost during the week. These repeated setbacks devastated her emotionally. "All of my good work this week is wasted," she would say. One day I wrote a few Affirmation Reminders and gave them to her to place in strategic areas of her home and car. She placed one on the refrigerator and one on her bedroom mirror. She also placed one on the dashboard of her car and one in the corner of her computer screen. The four cards read as follows:

"I'm going to be very happy on Monday because of my successful weekend."

"I only eat when I'm really hungry."

"My True Vision for weight loss is currently the most important thing in my life."

"I WILL maintain my weight over the weekend!"

That following weekend Kate told me that "a miracle occurred. I didn't gain a single pound this weekend." She told me that after using Affirmation Reminders she felt empowered to take on the weekend without that nagging anticipation of failure that always accompanied Friday's arrival. The Affirmation Reminder cards had worked the miracle! Instead of getting caught up in the activities of the weekend and pushing the habit of overeating to the back of her mind, these cards brought Kate's attention back to the one bad habit she really wanted to break.

I used Affirmation Reminders when building my two hundred-fifty store chain. I too would place them in key areas around my home and office to remind myself of what needed to be accomplished and for the sake of pure motivation. I gave Affirmation Reminders to all of my managers as well. When they would look at their computer screens they would see: "One hundred deliveries this month." "Being good to your customer's means being good to yourself." One of my favorites is one that I still use today: "Everything is difficult before it becomes easy." Affirmation Reminders serve an important purpose. They keep the mind focused on moving in the right direction. This in turn helps break a negative pattern and sets up the possibility of replacing that with a positive one. Affirmation Reminders keep us focused on not who we might be temporarily, but who we are able to become!

If you're going to use this powerful technique keep the following guidelines in mind:

1. **Repetition Works**—Place Affirmation Reminders in key areas of your house, office or wherever you spend the most time. This is because repetition is important. Seeing a message continually

has a greater impact on your mind. Do you realize that large corporations spend billions of dollars each year so that you will continually view their advertisements? This is one way that you can advertise—and internalize—the proper message to yourself. Take advantage of it by making sure you put the Affirmation Reminders in places where you will read them regularly. If you find yourself ignoring them after a while move them to a different location, or write new empowering messages.

2. **Be Positive**—State all of your Affirmation Reminders in the positive. If you're trying to lose weight, write: "I will lose 30 pounds," or "I see myself weighing 130 pounds." You would not state, "I will not gain more weight," as that is stated in the negative. We don't want to dwell on what needs to be avoided, but what we need to achieve. We always want to be forward thinking and positive, focusing on what action we want to take in order to help us form a Winning Habit and, of course, a winning end result.

3. **Proper Syntax**—Make sure that you are comfortable with how the Affirmation Reminder is worded, otherwise it will have a less powerful effect. If something is not written the way you would say it, rewrite it. You should be comfortable with that phrase or sentence and take complete ownership of it. This is more difficult to do when the words are not your own or not something you would say.

4. **Be Brief**—State precisely what you want in a clear concise manner. One short sentence will work better than a paragraph. Anything longer than one sentence should be written in your journal where it will do you more good in the long run.

Do you understand how powerful Affirmation Reminders can be? Do you see how they could help you? You can employ this technique with any negative habit that is causing you unhappiness and ultimately a long-term loss. You may not achieve success immediately, as Kate did, because sometimes it takes a little time for the message to become part of who you are. However, in the process of that happening, you're being reminded daily of who you want to become. Let's move on to other powerful techniques that will help you in achieving your True Vision!

The Five Ws Can Help You Define And Solve The Problem

Regardless of which habit you're attempting to break to fulfill your True Vision, use the five Ws to gather important information which will lead you to victory: Who, What, When, Where and Why.

For example, if you're trying to quit smoking, **Who** do you smoke with? There may be one person or a dozen people. Be honest and recollect exactly who these people are. **What** is the feeling, or short-term gain, you get from this experience? **When** precisely do you smoke? Is it in the morning, afternoon or evening? Is there a particular time of day when you smoke more? **Where** are you when you are doing the most smoking? Are you in your car? Are you at work? Are you in front of the television? Are you at the dinner table? Out with friends for the evening? There are usually a few key places. Finally, ask yourself this: **Why** am I smoking right now? I am asking you to be introspective in answering this question, but it's an important one. Are you nervous? Have you been drinking? Are you trying to be social and fit in? Is it the need for nicotine? What is your best assessment?

If you know that the only time you smoke is when you're around certain people, do you think you would smoke less if you spent less time around them? Do you think they would agree not to smoke when you are together? What if the majority of the cigarettes you smoked were with the same people and it took place between the hours of noon and four each afternoon? Do you see how certain places can be avoided or your behavior around certain people modified in order to achieve your True Vision?

Do you see how these same questions can help you regarding any bad habit you're attempting to break? You can overcome overeating, overspending, a gambling addiction, or virtually any other bad habit that stands in the way of accomplishing your True Vision. Once you have measured and monitored your habit and have an accurate profile of "who, what, when, where and why," you will be able to use this information to further focus on the specific habit that you want to eliminate. You will then be able to replace these bad habits with positive ones, which will ultimately propel you toward achieving your True Vision.

The Buddy System

If you're struggling to break free from a negative habit there is nothing better than having someone to assist you. Accountability is the key ingredient that makes this system so powerful and is the reason why some people hire personal trainers and life coaches. However, if you have a good friend who is struggling with the same problem, you can help each other!

With the Buddy System you become accountable to another human being, and he or she to you. Accountability demands that you do your very best: you don't want to let your buddy down or to look bad in front of him! Your buddy can be a relative, friend or co-worker. There is only one criterion that must be met before you use the Buddy System strategy. Make absolutely sure that this person is as sincere as you are in breaking free of this particular negative behavior. You don't want to ally yourself with someone who is not as serious as you are about succeeding or it may have the reverse effect of what you want. You may find yourself smoking more cigarettes per day, eating more of the wrong foods or heading generally in the opposite direction of your True Vision out of sheer frustration.

Once it is determined who your buddy will be, try to discuss your progress at least every week. Every day is even better. A good buddy will encourage her partner whenever possible and support her with positive comments. No one likes to hear a negative voice when trying to make important changes in life. If you're a good buddy, you have a better chance of having your partner be a good buddy in return. Make sure that neither of you becomes negative when temporary setbacks occur. Don't hold back when you meet with your buddy about your mutual problem. Tell your partner everything that has occurred relative to the habit you are trying to break. Encourage your buddy to do the same. Success is exciting. There is nothing more exciting than succeeding, unless it is succeeding with someone in a collaborative effort.

That is one reason that I believe strongly in any organization that promotes a unified attack against a negative habit. Some of the finest are Alcoholics Anonymous, Weight Watchers, and Gamblers Anonymous. There are many other clubs and organizations at both the local and national levels that are staffed by caring and trained individuals who can assist you. Whenever you bring a problem to the forefront of your mind and develop a plan to rid yourself of it, while simultaneously working shoulder to shoulder with others of similar interests, you have begun a powerful process. Activating that process will ultimately lead you to the elimination of the negative habit that has perhaps been stealing your money, your time, and your quality of life. I urge you now to take that first step and begin living that True Vision of the person that you really want to be!

chapter six

VISION STEP:
THE URGENCY FACTOR

Time is more valuable than money.
You can get more money,
but you cannot get more time.
   —Jim Rohn

Some find their motivation in books, others watch television and become very enthused. Many, however, commit the fatal error of not immediately acting on their idea. There may be certain things in their lives that are not going very well and they feel that they have to get them straightened out before beginning to work on their True Vision. How can I concentrate on my True Vision when I have this distraction going on? Does this sound like you? People who fall into this trap need to realize that they must act in the direction of their True Vision first, regardless of their distraction. Usually, when they do, the distraction often improves because of their efforts.

Let's consider, for example, a woman who refuses to work on her weight problem until she gets a good job. Sounds reasonable enough. But then she is neglecting the fact that she would have more energy and might be a much stronger candidate for a good job if she lost the forty pounds that she has always wanted to lose. **There's no question that victory breeds other victories. But first you must develop the Urgency Factor to take the immediate action you need to go out and get that first (or next) victory.**

Here Is One Million Dollars!

I developed the Urgency Factor mind-set while building my first large business. I think it can best be defined with the following example. If someone were to offer you one million dollars to make one important improvement in your life that you might have been putting off, could you do it? This challenge could be anything from losing weight, to starting a new career, to going back to school for the degree you have always wanted, to getting out of debt, or anything else that might be important to you. Could you do it for the lofty sum of one million dollars, or would you let the money slip through your hands? My bet is you would not only do it, but you'd be happy to do it! You would quickly develop a Vision for getting it done. You would see yourself accomplishing your mission and collecting the money. You would not fail! And so, that begs the question, why can't you do it anyway? Why does someone have to offer you an exorbitant amount of money for you to make a very positive change in your life? This change would most likely lead to more positive change; as I have repeatedly stated, victory breeds victory! Do you value the money over your own well-being and personal success? If you can do it for the money then we both know that you can do it for yourself.

What if you were to take on every challenge as though you were going to be paid one million dollars to get it done quickly and correctly? If you did that, you would then be using the Urgency Factor! And, if you used the Urgency Factor, for example, to build your wealth you would most likely have that million dollars and maybe far more!

The Urgency Factor is simply one more weapon in your success arsenal that must be employed in order for you to accomplish your True Vision. This particular technique is a most powerful tool. When growth was my Vision for my company, I opened new stores. I didn't just plod along thinking, "Oh well, looks like it's going to take longer than I thought." No way! If my plan was to open one new store per month, that is exactly what we did, no excuses and no delays. Eventually we opened one new store per week! This was done because we used the Urgency Factor and did not let time or distraction dictate how things would go. We grabbed time by the hands and ran for the finish line. And when I say "we" I mean just that. It was a total team effort, not unlike a tug of war team where everyone has to pull together or the mission is lost. What do you have in your life that would benefit from employing the Urgency Factor?

Time For A Vacation?

The Urgency Factor dictates many things. First, you can get more accomplished in less time than you think when you feel that you *have to*. For example, have you noticed how much more you can get done just prior to a vacation? If you know you cannot leave until you get certain things done, they get done. Isn't it odd how that works? What did you do differently? First of all, you cut out the distractions and moved along at a pretty fast pace. What are distractions? Prolonged conversations (are you concerned more about your social life than accomplishing your True Vision?), too many breaks during the day, oversleeping, staying out too late at night, long lunch breaks, chit-chat by the water cooler, dwelling on petty annoyances that will work themselves out anyway. The list is practically endless. Everyone has their own distractions; what are yours? What keeps you sidetracked?

Now is an excellent time to list your own time-wasting distractions which keep you from employing the Urgency Factor and accomplishing your True Vision. When it comes to your True Vision nothing of importance should ever be left undone, and I've found that people who are able to accomplish more things in one day than the average person have a better chance of succeeding at their True Vision. Make believe you are ready to go on vacation, but you must first accomplish certain things. Now do this every day and you will not only achieve your True Vision, but also be more likely to build additional success on top of that!

At my former company if a delivery needed to be made we didn't use the Shield of Excuse that there was not enough time on that particular day to schedule it. We used the Urgency Factor (the delivery has to be done today!) and got it done. Everyone was happy. The customer was happy because they received their order on time. And the store crew was happy because they were rewarded for growing their store. Our team became quite successful using this one technique.

You too can use the Urgency Factor in your life to accomplish your Vision. Remember, the Urgency Factor dictates that what you are attempting has your highest priority. All distractions must be set aside so that nothing of importance gets left undone. If you're beginning something then nothing will stop you from completion of that task. You'll be surprised at how much you can accomplish in a short period of time when there are no artificial barriers placed on you. When you act with urgency all things that pertain to your True Vision become important and you find yourself doing the amount of work in one day that used to take several days or even a week to accomplish. You'll be returning phone calls, making important contacts, and becoming more productive in meetings—in short, doing all of the tasks that need to be done in a shorter period of time—when you put the Urgency Factor to use.

Why am I so insistent that things be accomplished quickly? Because I have seen too many people fail because they become caught in a time warp. Do you know anyone like this? Time to them is a fuzzy concept; they're just plain pokey. They barely make it to work on time. They lose track of time. They treat time as if it is nonexistent. They always *plan* to get to it. The problem is that one day leads to another and nothing of significance gets accomplished. When you carry one day's activities over to a new day it gets easier to do the same thing again the following day. Sound familiar? These people start out the day moving at a snail's pace, accomplishing very little if anything at all. Then before they know it, it's time for lunch. The afternoon goes about the same way. The irony is that most of them have no idea that they are in a time warp. When you try to prod them along they think that something is wrong with you. "What's the rush, man?" The rush is, they have no respect for time and because of that one thing—yes, just because of that one "little" thing—they are missing the boat!

The truth is most people do have some kind of a Vision for their lives, but they never get around to working on it because they're always putting it off until a more opportune moment. Or, if they do perform a small bit of work on it, they overestimate their tiny accomplishment and sit back once again and settle in. Soon, the weeks have led to months, and the months to years, and before they know it, time runs out and nothing of significance has been done. Not because they couldn't have done it, but they failed for lack of exercising the Urgency Factor. Now, I'm sure you've heard the expression that there are no guarantees in life. Well, that's not exactly true. There are a few guarantees, and here is one: I guarantee that whatever the True Vision you have for your life, it will not be achieved if you don't employ the Urgency Factor. Don't be someone who fails because you have been caught in a time warp. Get going right now! If you do not have what you want, you need to respect the fact that time is running out. Get a hold of the Urgency Factor and understand that your personal success and wellbeing are far more valuable than one million dollars. You may have a Vision to make money, to lose weight, to find a new job—your Vision is more important than that one million dollars because it's about growing and becoming better than you are right now. Each one is about achieving your True Vision. That means that you win; depending on your True Vision that could mean physically or financially, but certainly you win emotionally. **If you think that being handed one million dollars feels better and is better for you than actually earning it, then you have neither earned a million dollars, nor been handed it!** When you employ the Urgency Factor it means that along the way you grow, learn new skills, and build incredible confidence until, before you know it, you get what you want. In the end you will feel like there is nothing you cannot do, increasing the scope of your True Vision and gaining far more than your original plan. You might just top the one million dollars in my example!

Time Is Our Most Important Resource

Time is not an unlimited resource. We squander it at our own peril. What are you waiting for? Why do you procrastinate? Each day that goes by without employing the Urgency Factor to make your True Vision a reality is one day lost. I know that one day may look like another: same surroundings, same traffic on the way to work, same people at work. Each new day resembles the previous one. In fact, I think that's one of the reasons that we all say "time flies." Since there doesn't seem to be any dramatic difference in our lives from one day to the next our minds tend to "lump" the days as if they are one. Before you know it a new month, year, or decade appears and we all think: "Where did the time go?" **Let's use time to our advantage because time is not on your side. It's like a wild stallion that must be corralled and tamed. Otherwise it will never serve you well.**

Our days fly too. We think we have sixteen productive hours in a day after removing the time we devote to sleep. However, if you take it a step further and remove the time we spend performing personal matters, we lose even more time. Eating takes up about two to three hours a day. Personal time with family and friends, time you spend brushing your teeth, going to the bathroom, making small talk with co-workers, and performing household tasks all take time. If you are a property owner you have to count yard work as well. These are things that may be necessary, but the hard fact is they don't get us any closer to achieving what we may really want in life, our True Vision. Taking away all of the time it takes to perform these functions reduces our productive time to about twelve hours or less per day. If you work an eight-hour day (and your current job is unrelated to your True Vision), that leaves you only about four hours for personal time. But that also leaves you about four hours to diligently work on your True Vision. The key is to do it, otherwise your dreams will be swept away by the passage of time. In fact, contrary to the popular expression, "Time is money," time is not money! You cannot save up time for later use. Nor can you borrow time from others to add to your own. Time is a critical factor that must be mastered in order for you to achieve your True Vision. You master time by using every precious second to your advantage. And you do this by employing the Urgency Factor!

Since you can't save time, borrow more, or stop time, make sure that you do all that you can with the time that you have. Let's begin to use the Urgency Factor by loading your day with potential mini-victories, taking action on one thing after another and avoiding all distractions. These steps do not have to be large. If your True Vision is to start a business, your task might be to make just one important phone call, and if your True Vision is weight loss, it could be a walk around the block. Set your agenda for daily victories and go out and accomplish every one of them. I want you to change your pace. If you find yourself at a temporary lull, rethink how you are employing the Urgency Factor. Maybe you're just plodding along and going with the flow like everybody else in that one area that you want so desperately to change. There's nothing wrong with this, if that's what you want in life. Many people live lives without a True Vision and seem content, at least outwardly. However, I'm thinking that you are currently reading this book because you're different. You have the desire to accomplish your True Vision. Your Vision may need to be refined and polished, but it's there peeking out at you from behind life's daily grind. So take action and develop the Urgency Factor so that you can make your Vision a reality!

Over-Analysis Leads To Paralysis

What if you're one of those people who have a natural tendency not to act? You may ponder, meditate and talk all about your True Vision but then nothing happens. Do you tend to over-analyze? Nothing can stop a good plan of action like over-analysis. Please don't misunderstand me. You need to fully understand your True Vision so that you can devise a plan to make it a reality. This often requires great thought and contemplation. There is a point, however, where the time for planning, talking and thinking must end and a time for taking action and employing the Urgency Factor begins. I caution you: over-analysis leads to paralysis!

One of my managers was the very best at planning his monthly in-store sales campaign. He had it all down to the last detail. I have no doubt that less time went into the planning of the invasion of Normandy! This guy was thorough. He painstakingly planned each step. He had lists of phone numbers. He had special in-store sales material he planned to put up. He even maintained special lists of former customers. He estimated floor traffic right down to the hour to make sure that the store was properly staffed. He would even analyze other competitor's specials that month. And of course the store sparkled like a shiny penny. When I first heard of this person's efforts I was impressed. "Here is a guy who really seems to get things done" I remember thinking.

You can imagine my surprise when at the end of the month his sales were not only not where I expected them to be, but were toward the bottom percentage of all our stores! "What happened?" I asked his supervisor. Well, what happened was the manager never stopped planning. He planned, organized and over-analyzed every important and insignificant detail. He thought of everything. The only problem was he did this right into the final day of the month and never took action on his plan. Month after month, while the store's objectives may have changed, his methods stayed the same. No one could ever get that guy to move beyond the planning and analysis stage. It would have been comical if it were not so frustrating.

Once again, I like planning and analysis. It's important to know where you are and how you are going to get to where you want to be. I'm not suggesting that you begin any project without understanding what you are facing. Details can make all the difference sometimes. But, if I had to choose between having a company full of analysts or a company loaded with doers, which do you think I would choose? I'll take those committed to the Urgency Factor every time! In the end the only way anything ever gets done, whether it be at a corporate level or in your personal life, is when you take action on a consistent basis. That means acting with Urgency!

Are You Afraid Of Failure?

Sometimes when a person is procrastinating or over-analyzing, it could be because they're afraid of a bad outcome. Some individuals play the wrong movie in their mind, the one that ends with failure. They play this scenario over and over again until they begin to believe it. Would you want to take action if you knew that you were going to fail? No one wants to fail. However, we know that the only way you will fail at anything you ever attempt is if you dare to take action. Interestingly, however, taking action is the only way that you succeed! It then makes sense that some of the biggest failures in life are also people who are some of the biggest winners as well. The more you try, the more you achieve both success and failure. Think about it: When has anyone ever failed at something that has never been tried? Have you ever seen anyone strike out in baseball from sitting on the bench? In fact, it can be said that the more you fail the more you are likely to eventually succeed, if you continue to change what is not working into something that does work. That takes repeated effort. Those who attach the word failure to themselves as opposed to their failing actions are creating a self-fulfilling prophecy (which I will talk about at length later in the book). If you try and your effort fails, you are not the failure; your actions have failed. That means that all you have to do is change what failed and try again. Keep in mind you are not the failure!

Have you ever heard the story of a man who spent five years devising machinery for mining iron ore? He later discovered that the machinery was too bulky to be practical. He also attempted on other occasions to construct an improved storage battery and to find a rubber source that was economical. All of these initiatives, and more, failed. Undeterred, he decided that the single-piece cast-concrete house was the wave of the future, along with concrete beds and other household furnishings made completely from concrete. This idea, like his others, failed miserably too. And you would never have heard of Thomas Alva Edison, the inventor of the incandescent light bulb, had he been afraid to fail! When an employee approached the great inventor and voiced concern over a recent failure, Edison replied: "Why man, I have not failed, I just have discovered thousands of things that won't work!" Edison refused to allow his failures to define him. He separated the two, knowing that with each try he got closer and closer to what would work. Do you cast yourself as a failure when it is really only your attempt that has failed?

Don't be afraid to employ the Urgency Factor because you might fail. In a recent survey it was found that it typically takes the average smoker seventeen serious attempts before he successfully kicks the habit! What would happen if you tried sixteen times and then gave up? Instead of fearing failure, welcome it as an additional learning experience. Don't take it personally. Your temporary failure has absolutely nothing to do with your long-term success, unless you stop trying. You are not a failure because your attempt failed. If for some reason your failed attempt is made public, those who would laugh at you because of your temporary set-back will only be that much more impressed when you arrive at your ultimate success. But if you quit because of your failed attempts, someday you are going to have regrets. So while I know it's difficult to keep acting with Urgency after you have a big let down, your efforts will only succeed if you continue to move forward!

Joe Padded His Failure

Some move through life never using the Urgency Factor to succeed so that they can feel better when they do fail. This twisted logic (that they seldom admit to themselves by the way) goes something like this: If you don't really try then you won't feel so bad about failing. After all, you never really gave it your best effort. In other words they begin with an actual backup plan to fail! I call this Padding Your Failure for a Softer Landing, as a soft landing won't hurt. This person is already attempting to make the failure more palatable by telling himself, "I never really had the chance to give it my best shot. If I had, I would probably have succeeded." Does this remind you of anyone you know? It reminds me of someone.

Several years ago an employee named Joe told me that he had always wanted his own business and now that he'd just turned 30 years of age he felt it was time to leave my company and start his own business, a service business involving lawn and garden care. While I knew

I was losing a valuable employee, I wished him the best. Joe thought of a great name for his new enterprise, acquired a van, expensive equipment, and went to a special school to learn the latest techniques concerning his new business. By this point, he had purchased several thousand dollars of equipment and had committed a great deal of time. He then did something that I found to be completely mystifying. He ran a tiny ad three times each week in the local newspaper and sat by the phone waiting for it to ring. Not wanting to see him fail, I asked him to stop by my office and attempted to point out a better marketing approach—hey, *any* marketing approach. Where was the news release of a new business opening? A local newspaper would have run a story for free. Why didn't he have a flyer printed up and hand-delivered to homeowners who could use (and afford) his services? For that matter why didn't he make the tiny ad that he was running into a coupon that offered great savings if you acted now? There are many more ways to promote a new business which cost nothing, or practically nothing.

I had several meetings with Joe covering all of this and more. Finally, I loaned him some materials from my library describing successful marketing techniques. This was all to no avail. It was sad hearing about Joe sitting in his rented office day after day waiting for the phone to ring. It did ring occasionally, but not enough to help the business catch on. As the days passed, Joe became more and more depressed. He continued to re-play what had been the mental failure movie until he finally quit. He ended up liquidating his equipment for less than half of what he paid for it. That was the end of Joe's entrepreneurial adventure as he went to work for a competitor shortly thereafter.

In retrospect what occurred isn't hard to figure out. The day Joe gave up it was as if a cloud had lifted from his head. He was happy and smiling. And what he said explained it all: "I really didn't have enough money to make a business like that work anyway." In other words, Joe was "padding his failure." The reason that he failed had little to do with start-up capital. It had everything to do with not having the Urgency Factor, and a solid True Vision for success. Most of the marketing ideas that I gave Joe were actually free, or cost very little. However, had he taken action and done these things he would not have had as soft a landing had he still failed. He would have publicly been associated with his business. He would have committed himself one hundred percent to success and everyone would have known it! He was quite good at protecting himself from a personal and public failure. He was not at all good at building a business that would have made him financially independent.

Are You Afraid To Succeed?

One more reason why some of us don't take enough action to succeed is fear. Some of us may actually be afraid to succeed. Success and failure, while being at the extreme ends of the spectrum and seemingly opposite in every way, do in fact have at least one similarity. Whether you succeed or fail you have separated yourself from the group. You are no longer one of the gang. And, unconsciously, you may be connecting some sort of negative consequence to being unlike your friends, acquaintances, or family members. Change—any change—makes you somewhat different than your peer group. Therefore, you could be thinking that people will be holding you to a higher standard because of your success. If you succeed at making your True Vision a reality you may worry that you are now going to be expected to succeed at everything you attempt. When you do this, you undermine your Vision and sabotage the movie that is constantly running before your mind's eye.

Sometimes we scare ourselves into inaction by the concern that others might be envious of our success. Are you concerned that others will be jealous of your accomplishments? While this sometimes happens, most of the time real friends are truly happy that you've gotten what you wanted in life. Sure, there will be those who try to degrade your achievements. Sometimes those who do not rise with us seem smaller in their own eyes. When this happens, those insecure people attempt to push you back down to the small standard by which they judge themselves. Their subconscious directs them, "If I can't do it then neither can she." **Just remember this: they only win when you stop succeeding, not when you start!**

More importantly, the people who really matter in your life don't act that way. Those who do lash out are not really friends, and probably never were. The good news is that when they're completely out of your life, you'll have more time for better relationships, relationships with those who truly do care about you and will indeed be happy for any future success.

George Herbert, an English clergyman and poet, said it best: "Living well is the best revenge." Envy has been a part of human nature since Cain slew Abel. It will continue to be a part of human nature as long as people inhabit the earth. If you let people stop you from using the Urgency Factor in achieving your True Vision and becoming all that you are capable of being, then *they* have truly won. I don't believe that you're going to let that happen. After all, you've already exercised the Urgency Factor by purchasing this book and reading this far, haven't you? There is absolutely nothing stopping you from going all the way!

Needless Guilt

Finally, one more thing that may prevent you from activating the Urgency Factor is when you don't really feel you deserve success. The logic goes something like this: "Look at all of the starving people in the world, and I have so much," or, "My mother tried for years to lose weight, and couldn't do it. What gives *me* the right to succeed?"

Get the idea? Let's take a closer look at these feelings. True, there are many starving people in the world. Do you want to help them? I mean really help them? Then make a lot of money! When you do this you are helping a greater number of people. You are helping all of the people whom you employ, and all of the people who are employed by businesses where your employees spend their money. This is capitalism at its most basic, and it works! In addition, the more money you have, the more you can directly help those who are less fortunate. An admirable model for this is the Bill and Melinda Gates Foundation, the largest charitable foundation in the world, which gives away about 1 billion dollars annually! I suppose that Bill Gates could have felt guilty after making his first million dollars, but look at all of the people he is able to help because he continued using the Urgency Factor to maximize his business skills and never allowed guilt to deter him. You too should certainly assist the disadvantaged to the extent that you are able. My point is, however, that you can do much more if you have more. It's difficult to assist someone up to the next financial level when you are also on his or her level. Don't let unnecessary guilt prevent you from using the Urgency Factor to make your True Vision a reality!

Don't feel guilty about others who have tried and failed, who are close to you. Maybe they never had a True Vision for success the way you do. Maybe they didn't use the proper techniques, perhaps they didn't work smart. As we have seen there's a big difference between working hard and working smart. If you were attempting to till an area of dirt to put in a garden, and began by using a spoon and working all day every day until the sun went down, I would say that you're a hard worker. However, you are not working smart, are you? Better that you obtain the proper tools and go to work in a methodical manner. You'll finish faster and do a better job. Big difference! How does this apply to you?

Maybe when your Mom tried to lose weight she went on a fad diet. Fad diets rarely bring lasting results. You, on the other hand, have created your own True Vision and applied the proper Vision Steps, and you deserve success! And, most likely, that person you are feeling guilty about will likely be happy when you achieve success. And, if they don't, my question to you is this: whose life is it anyway? If you're struggling with a weight problem you owe it not only to yourself, but also to those you love and who depend on you, to be as healthy as possible. Don't let needless guilt prevent you from taking action and employing the Urgency Factor to make your True Vision a reality!

You need to adopt the Urgency Factor and take action toward your True Vision today! You also need to continue to use the Urgency Factor until you achieve your True Vision, even if it means beginning again, and again. Everyone fails (I certainly have), but don't worry about it; failure is only temporary if you just keep moving forward. Success once achieved, on the other hand, can be permanent. If you're having a problem taking that first step, go back and work on your True Vision. There is a good chance you are missing something. If not you would be raring to go. When your Vision is clear and strong, begin again. Success could mean giving your True Vision just one more try!

What could you do right now to take one more step toward accomplishing your True Vision? Remember, we just want one small victory, as victory breeds more victory. Is there one phone call that you should make? Is there one person that you could speak to? Is there one place that you should go? What step are you currently able to take right now that you may have been putting off until a later date? Only you can answer that question. I encourage you to take that first step. You don't know for sure how long your journey will take until it's complete; however, you will never complete your journey and fulfill your True Vision until you take that next step! What step should you take right now?

chapter seven

VISION STEP: TOTAL FOCUS

Success demands singleness of purpose.
  —Vincent Lombardi

A Powerful Secret?

There is one technique that seems at once to be so clear yet so misunderstood that people almost forget to consider it. It's not really a secret, but it might as well be one. And yet, regardless of your ability, intelligence level, social or economic status, or almost anything else, this one technique can change the course of your life. It's called Total Focus.

Let's look first at the obvious. We can all agree that when we neglect something it usually gets worse. If you neglect your spouse your relationship will worsen. If you neglect your car it won't run as well. If you neglect your job you may get fired. So it is with just about everything within your sphere of influence. I'm sure we can agree that things get better not by accident, but by design. If you look at just these examples—your marriage, your car, your job—I'm sure you can imagine how each would improve by even temporarily using Total Focus. Will your spouse be upset if you dote on him or her? Funny, I've never seen anyone become upset and draw away from someone they love because that person was paying them special attention. This same principle applies broadly as well. **Whatever we focus on in life expands and whatever we neglect contracts.**

When you give something your Total Focus you're telling yourself that it's indeed important and its importance grows even greater as you continue to focus on it. That sounds simple yet I've found that many people have a difficult time mastering it. Sometimes the reason is that this technique demands that you eliminate distractions from your life. There are almost always things that you currently think of as important, but in reality are not. Consider your commitments. For example: if you're a member of a Thursday night bowling league, is that helping you achieve your True Vision, or is it a distraction? Certainly, if your Vision is to become a better bowler, then it helps. Short of that, if you're utilizing Total Focus then bowling is a distraction from time that could be spent making your True Vision a reality. **That is, anything that pulls you away from your True Vision will not help you achieve it.** Think about this: how much time do you spend surfing the Internet, Twittering, texting friends, or talking on the phone? I'm not advocating that you have to live like a monk in order to employ Total Focus. What I am suggesting is that there are things in life that are distracting and have the power to pull us away from, instead of closer to, our True Vision. Sometimes all it takes is for us to become overly occupied with far less important matters on a regular basis.

When you practice Total Focus you are placing your Vision above all else. You are making it not just some vague priority, but are giving it a reality of its own. Giving your Vision Total Focus means giving your time and energy to your True Vision, regardless of what else in your life you may like to do or think needs attention. You are focusing all, or most, of your attention and energy on your Vision, and that is what makes this technique so powerful! You are in essence saying that your True Vision is the most important thing in your life, making just about everything else secondary. I'm not suggesting that you use this technique for an extended period of time, although some people will sacrifice massive amounts of time to see their True Vision through. But Total Focus is an excellent way to either launch your True Vision or to kick-start it if it seems to be stalled.

When you act with Total Focus think of yourself as similar to a laser beam. You can have 100 light bulbs in a room all lighted at the same time, yet other than both the room temperature and your electric bill rising, little else will take place. **If you take that same wattage,** however, and turn it into a laser beam, you'll be able to burn a hole through the wall of that room. This is what I mean by Total Focus!

Try this experiment: On a sunny day go outside with a magnifying glass. Focus it over an old newspaper and don't move, keep it on that one spot. Before long a fire will begin. You've just harnessed the power of the sun by using Total Focus! Now think about what would have happened if you moved the magnifying glass back and forth instead of holding it focused over one spot. There would have been no fire. The fact that you used Total Focus on that one specific area gave you the power to create fire by using the sun as a source. When we have Total Focus almost nothing is impossible for us to achieve.

The Rudolph's—An Amazing Story Of Total Focus

The following story is a true testimony to Total Focus, a real life example of human beings going above and beyond, focusing on one of the most important matters in their life, the health of their child. Wilma Rudolph, an African American, was the 20th of 22 children. She was born in Clarksville, Tennessee on June 23, 1940. A premature baby weighing only 4 pounds at birth, at age four she was stricken with scarlet fever, double pneumonia, and polio, which later required her to wear a heavy metal brace on one of her legs. Sadly, she was bedridden most of the time and would watch the other kids playing outside her window. Her only desire at that time was to be able to play and run with the other children.

Her parents, Ed and Blanche Rudolph, were hardworking but very poor. Mr. Rudolph worked as a railroad porter and handyman. Mrs. Rudolph did cooking, laundry, and housekeeping. In spite of a very challenging financial condition Wilma's mother was determined to help her daughter try to live a normal life and she did so with Total Focus!

Each morning Blanche would first massage Wilma's legs and then encourage her to do exercises. One can only imagine the pain that young Wilma felt each time that she went through her exercise session, but she continued on at the urging of her mother. In addition, for seven years she and her mother made weekly 100-mile treks for treatments on her leg. Some months it was difficult to notice any progress at all, but they persisted with Total Focus and slowly but steadily the treatments began to work. By the age of 11 Wilma could finally walk without braces on her legs. But she didn't stop there. A strange thing happened. Rather than just keeping up with the other kids, she started to outrun them.

The Total Focus that Blanche had for her daughter's recovery was passed on to Wilma, who continued training hard even after she could walk and run. She became such a good athlete she starred on her high school basketball team, setting state records for scoring and leading her team to a state championship. But she didn't stop there; she now had a strong True Vision for athletics.

She became a champion on her school track team. In fact she was so good by the age of 16 she began training seriously for the 1956 Olympics! Wilma not only made the team but actually won a Bronze medal. But even that achievement wasn't good enough for Wilma, whose training regimen was legendary at that point. At the age of 20, Wilma Rudolph entered the 1960 Olympics and the former crippled, sickly child became the first African American woman ever to win three gold medals!

This impressive story epitomizes many things in this book, not the least of which is Total Focus. Few of us can say that we have greater obstacles to overcome than Wilma Rudolph. Wilma had virtually everything against her, yet succeeded anyway. She was an African American born at a time when racism was far worse than it is today. She was poverty stricken and 1 of 22 children. In addition to all of that, she had to overcome a disability by traveling 100 miles each week for physical therapy! Sometimes we don't know how fortunate we are with the challenges that lie before us until we see someone else who has to overcome even larger obstacles.

By exercising Total Focus, Self-Discipline, Winning Habit, the Urgency Factor and, of course, having a True Vision, Wilma Rudolph became and remains today an American hero.

What is your True Vision? How much Total Focus are you willing to direct toward its accomplishment? **I suggest to you that instead of spreading your attention across many different areas you concentrate on your True Vision with intensity and Total Focus.** This means that you must set aside other priorities temporarily and give your particular Vision Total Focus. Do you understand the power of this one technique? While you may not be able to use this particular tool for an extended time period (although the Rudolph's used it for 7 years during Wilma's therapy), you will most assuredly get a head start by beginning the process with this one technique. Get a jump on your True Vision with Total Focus!

Focus On The Right Things

It's very important that you understand every aspect of what you are trying to accomplish. Since what you focus on will expand, make sure that you're focusing on the right things. Measure, monitor and study exactly how to accomplish your True Vision. The technique of Total Focus in its most basic form is all about directing large amounts of time, effort and energy toward your True Vision.

For example, if your True Vision is weight loss, I want you to make sure you know exactly how much weight you want to lose and that you have all of the tools necessary for your success. A scale is an essential tool because you want to make sure that you weigh yourself regularly. It astounds me how many people say they are attempting to lose weight, and yet don't even know how much they weigh because they don't own or have access to a good scale. Even worse, they're afraid to know exactly how much they actually weigh. This sounds like neglect, which if you recall is the opposite of Total Focus. Not having the proper tools to accomplish your True Vision is like a carpenter going to work without his hammer and saw. You need the proper tools to get the job done.

If weight loss is your True Vision, expand your knowledge of the entire topic. Learn how many calories are in one jelly doughnut, a Twinkie, or any other food that you know you shouldn't be eating. You should know how many calories are burned when you walk one mile at your current body weight. On the other hand, how many calories does a person your size burn each day without exercising? Remember the five Ws we talked about? **Who** are the people you are with when you overeat? **What** specific food(s) are you eating that cause weight gain? **When** are you most vulnerable to binge eating? **Where** are you located when you are eating the wrong foods? **Why** do you feel the need to eat when you know you're not hungry? If weight loss is your True Vision, then you need to know the particulars that will help you achieve that Vision. Become an expert at knowing all the facts involved in your quest. No great Vision becomes a reality without a complete understanding of the many factors involved. How can you use Total Focus if you don't know what to focus on? **Success rarely happens by accident. It takes a purposeful, passionate effort using all of the information and tools that are available.**

What Do You Focus On?

I believe that some people don't get out of life what they want primarily because they don't know what they want. In other words, they don't know what to focus on. Does this make sense? If you drive away in your car not knowing where to go you might end up anywhere. Just driving without a set destination might be fun for a Sunday afternoon, but it's not the best way to live your life. A person who has no idea what to focus on will usually end up with nothing or very little. If you don't have a Vision for maintaining a lean athletic body then it would be easy for someone to pull you into eating doughnuts with them each morning. Those who are not focused on living smoke free will quickly accept a cigarette offered to them by a co-worker. Those who are not able to hang on to a dollar and consequently live beyond their means have never bothered to map out a logical path that would lead them to financial independence or at least to a debt free existence. Many people just seem to bounce around from one idea to another, getting pulled into other people's plans and actions, because they don't seem to have a solid Vision of their own. You first need to develop a True Vision for what you really want, and then use Total Focus to help you achieve it!

Total Focus is so powerful it can even trump genetics when it comes to building great athletes, musicians, chess players, writers and other highly talented professionals. In his book *Outliers* Malcolm Gladwell states that, "Ten thousand hours is the magic number of greatness." In order to apply Total Focus to anything for 10,000 hours you must commit three hours a day, every day, for just over 9 years! But don't be intimidated. Your True Vision may be more modest than to "change the world." You will probably not need anywhere near that amount of time in order to achieve your True Vision. However, success at any endeavor does require Total Focus at some level. As Gladwell tells us, "Practice isn't the thing you do once you're good. It's the thing you do that makes you good."

Are you willing to Totally Focus on your True Vision? Do you understand how this powerful Vision Step will supercharge your efforts? This one technique can virtually change the course of your life, regardless of your ability, intelligence level, social or economic status, or anything else. I assure you, whatever you decide to give your Total Focus to will vastly improve!

chapter eight

VISION STEP:
EFFECTIVE COMMUNICATION

Life's most important battles are won between your two ears!
—Bob Natoli

How To Talk To Yourself

The first and most important form of communication is what occurs within you. Many times people give up before they even begin because they convince themselves that whatever lies before them cannot be accomplished. When they do this they are practicing poor self-communication techniques. After all, what is thinking but inner communication? Does your inner voice fill you with inspiration or hold you back with negative chatter? If you're going to make your True Vision a reality you have to be able to control your thought process to the point where you can differentiate between harmful and helpful inner communication.

Any negative phrase if repeatedly thought will be believed. "I'll never be able to lose thirty pounds, who am I kidding?" "The boss doesn't like me and won't pick me for that promotion." "I've smoked all of my life and I will probably die with a cigarette in my hand." This type of inner communication is dangerous for many reasons. It depletes your reserve of positive energy. But this kind of repeated inner chatter can create something called a self-fulfilling prophecy. Sociologist Robert K. Merton first used the term "self-fulfilling prophecy" in his book *Social Theory and Social Structure*. Merton essentially reasons that any prediction not necessarily based on fact which is believed by the predictor (you) may eventually end up as the truth simply because he or she actually believed that it would happen. You don't want to set yourself up for failure so be very careful what you say to yourself as a prediction of doom and gloom may just come true because you have predicted it! (More on this in Chapter Nine).

Remember that movie that's always playing in the theater of the mind? When we speak in an overly harsh manner to ourselves we're replaying that negative movie over and over. This form of inner communication stops us in our tracks. **How many times have you been halted from achieving your True Vision because you could not still that negative voice? Walk out on your inner negative movie just as you would in a real theater!**

How To Be Realistic

When you practice negative inner communication you're not being realistic, but rather fearful and self-defeating. You're usually making an unfounded negative prediction with insufficient or wrong information regarding a future event. For example, when you tell yourself, "I'll never be able to lose thirty pounds, who am I kidding?" you are presumably communicating this thought to yourself because you have not been able to lose this amount of weight—yet. Does this mean that you won't be able to lose that amount of weight? No. It just means that as yet you have not been able to lose that amount of weight. What you need to realize is that by repeatedly communicating to yourself in this way you reinforce a false belief, and if reinforced enough times it will become fact. It becomes fact if for no other reason than you believe it to be true. Your self-communication ultimately determines the course of your actions. Why would anyone pursue a True Vision for their life if they knew ahead of time that it wouldn't be possible to succeed?

I'm not asking you to walk around with your head in the clouds. On the contrary, I want you to be more realistic. When you communicate words such as "never" or "always" you are not using words that are accurate. When you do, you're drawing a sweeping conclusion that is usually inaccurate, and certainly unproven. Rephrase, "I will never be able to lose thirty pounds, who am I kidding?" into: "Maybe I have not found the right way yet but I know I can lose thirty pounds, many have lost much more." What a difference! Which statement makes more sense? The first statement is a sweeping conclusion that is not based on fact. The second statement is realistic and it also makes you feel like you *can* achieve the loss of thirty pounds. By changing the words, you can change how you feel about your own possibility of success. **The change in your inner communication results in a change in your emotion and ultimately your actions, raising your chances of attaining a positive end result!**

No longer rely on the tired old phrases and negative words that have stopped you from achieving your True Vision. Thinking in broad negative terms is not only inaccurate but also defeatist. As with any change, you need to gradually recondition your self-communication techniques. I'm not asking you to immediately stop the way you've been communicating to yourself for all these years. However, try to be aware the next time you're communicating a negative phrase to yourself; immediately think afterwards in more upbeat and accurate language. Never let an inaccurate negative inner communication be the final word—immediately rephrase it. After a short time you'll be amazed at how your inner communication will improve. Eventually, you will be communicating appropriately with no correction needed.

Inner Communication

Below is a list of self-defeating internal communications. Next to it is a list of more accurate thoughts. The most important thing is to be realistic. It is not my mission to change you into a wide-eyed optimist. However, what I do want is for you to communicate with yourself more accurately. When you do, you will not be held back by your inner critic. In fact, you'll be encouraged by the positive reality of your situation. You'll make a new beginning. Beginnings are the first step in turning your True Vision into a reality!

Defeatist, broad-ranging, all or nothing, one-sided, inaccurate statements:	Positive, but accurate statements:
"This is too hard, I can't do it."	"This might be tough but everything is difficult before it is easy."
"I have smoked all of my life and I can't quit now."	"It will be difficult in the beginning, but I can quit smoking. Many people have done it!"
"My mother, sister and all of my aunts are overweight. That's just the way I am built."	"My mother, sister and aunts are all overweight. They also overeat and never exercise. The difference is I will eat healthy and follow an exercise plan."
"I didn't come from money and I won't end up with money."	"Eighty percent of all millionaires in America are self-made. They didn't inherit their money, they did it themselves and so can I."
"I will never lose weight. I have a slow metabolism."	"If I begin a weightlifting program my metabolism will speed up. Muscle burns calories faster than fat. Then I will lose as much weight as I want."
"I am sick of trying to quit smoking. This is the tenth time I have tried."	"The average smoker attempts to quit seventeen times before he succeeds. I think I can do it in fewer tries."
"My husband/wife spends so much money we will never get out of debt."	"It won't be easy, but we can get out of debt if we stop spending more than we make."

Are you getting the idea? *You must first communicate with yourself in an accurate, positive manner before any real change for the better can take place.* Now, take out a sheet of paper and write down the sort of communication you've been practicing with yourself. Write exactly what you have been thinking and next to it write down your new phrase. Every time you communicate with yourself in a negative, unrealistic manner, rephrase it in the new, accurate, positive way. For each defeatist, broad-ranging, all or nothing statement, write one positive but accurate statement about the same thing. In the beginning you may not really believe the new positive statement, but in time you will, just as it took time for you to believe the negative sweeping conclusion. Use the Urgency Factor and do this exercise right now while you're thinking about it. The book will be here waiting when you return.

How we communicate with ourselves is <u>the</u> most important form of communication! It is what creates that never-ending movie that plays in our mind. This also makes self-communication the single most important means of establishing and ultimately achieving your True Vision!

Getting It Straight From The Start

When you communicate with others do you do so with confidence? Do you look them in the eye? Do you speak with expression in your voice? Do you smile when it's appropriate? Do you always carefully communicate all of your important points? When we have True Vision it's extremely important that at the proper time we communicate appropriately with others in the most effective manner possible. What you're looking for from other people is the same thing that they are looking for from you, to be understood.

I developed the next Vision Step, "**Getting It Straight From The Start**," to clearly demonstrate that it's your responsibility to make sure that whomever you speak with understands exactly what you want. It's the responsibility of the communicator to make sure that the message is not only heard but is also completely understood.

There are some people who will always hear what they want to hear. Have you ever said something like this to your teenager? "I want you to pick up your room and do all of your homework and then I will take you to the movies tonight with two of your friends." When the evening rolls around the child asks you what time you are going to pick up her friends as she has already telephoned them and started making the arrangements. When you ask about the condition of her room and if all of her homework has been completed, she flashes you a look like a deer caught in a car's headlights, wide eyed, gaping mouth. "I hung my jacket up like you told me to." Then she becomes a little agitated. "Oh come on, you never told me the rest of the deal! Besides, I didn't have much homework anyway, and I can do it tomorrow morning. This isn't fair!" See how easy it is to suddenly become the bad guy?

What happened in this example is simple. The mom was not completely heard by her daughter. This is because her daughter heard what she wanted to hear. We all have the tendency to do this at every age with things that we most love, or most fear. An employee is liable to hear, "I promise you a one thousand dollar bonus no matter what," when in fact the boss may have attached a certain sales quota or other qualifier to the bonus in a subtle manner. Conversely, an employee can become quite shaken if he or she hears of imminent layoffs even though his supervisor told him that he would not be affected by the layoffs. Discussions that trigger concerns and emotions, even when they may not directly affect that particular person, may still be unsettling if not communicated properly by **Getting It Straight From The Start**. Our fears, in this case of being fired, can sometimes trigger our mental movie to play a double feature with us as the person being fired, and then not being able to afford a nice Christmas for the kids. With many other sacrifices sure to follow, this creates a most unpleasant picture. We edit our mental movie with the things we love and the things we fear, as each of these offer either great attraction or repulsion. Certain key words and phrases that we hear help create these very vivid mental pictures.

One more stumbling block to proper communication is the fact that we tend to reduce what we hear into small easily understood sound bites that make sense to us. We streamline information as we hear it, without even realizing that we do it. That teenaged daughter wanted to go to the movies with her friends and was so overjoyed at hearing she could that she reduced the entire message to, "Hang up your jacket, and then I'll take you and your friends to the movies." She was so fixated upon the words "go to the movies" that the other part of the message, which was far less important to her, was lost. Since we all think in pictures and not in words, the teen cut to an immediate mental snapshot of her and her friends enjoying themselves at the movies, as this was her desire, what she really wanted to do.

This is why the technique of **Getting It Straight From The Start** is important to all of us, at every level, especially as we have more people to communicate with. In 1984 when "the Great Communicator," President Ronald Reagan, was running for re-election, he had a reputation as a "hawk," someone who is not afraid to resort to the use of military force. Since this was the case, his chief strategic advisors informed him that he could never say the words "nuclear war" unless he also said "must not be fought and can never be won." The advisors wisely determined that some voters, especially those who already feared his "hawkish" stance, would hear what they wanted to hear, unless the words were phrased properly. They understood that it only takes an instant to envision a mushroom cloud of nuclear dust destroying everything for miles. It would have been a fatal mental image to attach to Reagan's re-election bid. As previously stated, human beings simply muster a more vivid mental picture of certain things that tug on their emotions through great attraction or great revulsion.

We need to communicate a clear message so that our listener has no opportunity to use any sort of built-in bias and walk away with the wrong meaning.

Mom Needs To Get It Straight
From The Start And So Do You

Mom needed to Get It Straight From The Start. She should have looked her teenage daughter straight in the eye when there were no distractions, and spoken clearly and precisely the following in a firm though pleasant sounding tone (more on voice inflection later in the book): "I would like you to do two things for me," she might have said. "First I want you to pick up all of the clothes in your room, fold them neatly and place them in your dresser. The second thing I would like you to do is to complete your Social Studies and English homework. If you get both of these things done by 6:00 p.m. I'm going to reward you by taking you and your friends to the movies. Remember, honey, if you don't get the job done there will be no movies."

The difference between this example and the previous one is obvious. First, the mother carefully listed each item she wanted completed at the beginning of the conversation. Then, if these specific things were accomplished by the designated time, the daughter would be rewarded by going to the movies with her friends. As a final warning the mother restated that if the job wasn't done, she would rescind the movie offer. And while she did this, the mother should have maintained constant eye contact with her teen. I have observed over the years that more of my message was remembered when eye contact was involved as opposed to having my listener being even slightly distracted by looking away.

You are in essence attempting to overcome a listener's natural tendency to oversimplify your message and hear what he or she wants to hear. You are also making your message and its consequences perfectly clear so your listener will be unable to feign confusion at a later date.

Always use the following tools so that you get it straight from the start:

- Make eye contact.
- Use the proper tone and voice inflection.
- Be specific with your message regarding dates, times and basic details.
- Restate your message in different words if there is any question about their meaning (and sometimes even when there is no question).
- Make sure words that carry a natural attraction or repulsion are used carefully and appropriately.

There are some who fail to achieve their True Vision merely because of poor communication skills. If this has happened to you in the past do not feel badly. We've all had this happen at one time or another. The difference is from this point forward you're not going to be that type of person. You are going to know what you want and you are going to be able to communicate it in an effective manner! If you have True Vision only you can stop your success! Keep in mind when people know exactly what you want, you have a far better chance of actually getting it.

Are Your Feelings Accurately Represented?

It's easy to remember when you're on the wrong end of poor communication. Remember the last time you were in a restaurant and the waiter or waitress asked you what you wanted to order? She stood there with eyes gazing off into space or looking down, barely speaking audibly with a monotonous voice. She displayed little enthusiasm for the job, and certainly not in taking your order. You may not have attributed this behavior to poor communication skills but that is most likely what it was. She was acting as though she didn't care whether you ordered dinner or left the restaurant. While some people really don't care one way or the other, I've found that many times this type of person does in fact care, but is not aware of how they look or sound. Consequently, they communicate an inaccurate message without even knowing it.

I had an employee at our corporate office with this problem. Dennis was an exceptional worker, but turned off his staff with poor communication skills. The people who worked directly under him constantly received the wrong message. Dennis had a very serious demeanor and a face that conveyed very little emotion. When he wanted something accomplished by a member of his staff he would speak in hushed tones and look past them in an odd way. This made him seem like he was talking down to them. In Dennis's mind, he was merely relaying what he wanted using as few words as possible. However, in the minds of his staff he was a cruel, emotionless machine.

One morning one of his female staff members asked to see me. As soon as she was seated in front of my desk she began to cry. Naturally, I immediately asked what was wrong. I braced myself as I expected to hear a horror story regarding some sort of abuse. She said, "I can't work for Dennis anymore." "What did he do?" I replied. "He is an awful person," she cried out. "Awful?" I repeated, puzzled. "What exactly happened, tell me." I leaned forward in my chair expecting the worst. "I don't know, he's just mean and I can't take it anymore." I continued to ask the woman for details but none were forthcoming.

I asked another member of Dennis's staff into my office to see if that person could shed any light on the subject. When he arrived I heard the same sort of story. Finally, I personally interviewed every one of Dennis's five-member team. While none were as upset as this one woman, every one of them disliked Dennis. No one could give me any damning evidence, other than to say that they would prefer not to work for him. As I reflected on what I'd heard it seemed Dennis's communication techniques had done him in. There had been too many steely glares, too little emotion and zero empathy displayed.

It was a sad day when I had to remove Dennis from his position. This may seem unfair to the reader, but you can't have someone in a position of authority who is not able to show empathy and understanding or to communicate effectively with those he manages. At least that's not how a good company should run. Poor communication techniques lead to mixed messages, low productivity, hurt feelings, and low morale. When I called Dennis into my office he was as surprised as I have ever seen anyone. He couldn't imagine that his staff felt as they did. At first he thought I was using this as an excuse to remove him from his position. I actually had to ask for volunteers from his team to step into my office so that they could convey their feelings to him personally. I still have a very vivid picture of him sitting in my office staring at the floor emotionless. "I thought they liked me, I liked them. I can't believe that I come off this way," he said, still displaying no emotion. The picture that Dennis had of himself as an effective leader was just not accurate. While not necessarily true, he was viewed as a curmudgeon. I temporarily placed Dennis in a position where he worked more with paper and numbers than with people. Eventually, I had the opportunity to work with him and he vastly improved his communication skills.

Are you perceived accurately? If you're going to fulfill your True Vision you need to be able to communicate exactly what you want while leaving others with a good feeling about who you are. Let's look at some **Effective Communication techniques**, and consider why they're important and how they work.

Eye Contact

Looking into the eyes of the person to whom you are speaking is one of the most powerful techniques that you can use when communicating. How did you feel the last time that you had a conversation with someone, and that person is looking everywhere but into your eyes? In fact, looking everywhere, except into a person's eyes is almost a cliché for guilt. Think about little Johnny who just threw a ball through the kitchen window. When confronted he looks at his fingers, gazes at the ceiling, stares into your belt buckle but rarely looks directly into your eyes. The perception: Guilty as charged! You don't want to appear guilty when in fact you're trying to make a good impression.

But neither is it a good idea to stare intently and endlessly into someone's eyes. That can be regarded as intimidating (if not strange). Have you ever seen two individuals who are about to engage in a fist-fight? The very first thing they do, depending upon how physically close they are to each other, is to lock eyes. Each is first attempting to dominate the other person with this form of communication by waiting for the other person to look away. This strategy helps a person prove to himself that he is the dominant one. You can also see this if you watch boxing or mixed martial arts matches. The fighters are routinely in the center of the ring trying to stare each other down as the referee reads the rules. At least this is the way it usually works.

A strange example of this, because it had a different twist, took place a few years ago, involving a mixed martial arts fighter named

Heath Herring. Herring, a 6'4", two-hundred fifty pound, mixed martial arts fighter nicknamed "The Texas Crazy Horse," was face to face staring down the man he was about to do battle with in the middle of the ring. Suddenly, his opponent leaned forward and ever so gently kissed Herring right on the lips! I happened be watching this match and I couldn't believe my eyes. As soon as he was kissed, Herring threw a vicious right-cross knocking the other fighter to the floor and into a more serious delirium than he was already in. Perhaps Herring's opponent was trying to add a bizarre new twist to stare-down ritual in the center of the ring. I have no idea, but it was the strangest "stare-down" that I've ever seen. Anyway, if you're not about to get into a fight with someone don't stare intently into his eyes. If you are about to fight with someone certainly don't kiss him—from what I saw that was a really bad strategy. Establish proper eye contact, gaze naturally at the person's eyes, then subtly drift away and back again.

Proper eye contact will always get you off to a good start regardless of what you're trying to achieve. In turn, when you're searching people for correct answers, remember to first check their eyes. If they're trying to avoid eye contact with you they may have something to hide. If their eyes are blinking rapidly, they may either be insecure or possibly attempting to hide something as their mind races to think of their next misleading statement. Of course they could have something in their eye, or have a natural facial tic; there's always that possibility. There will be more on this later in the book when we discuss "The 12 Sure Fire Signs That You Are Being Lied To!"

Other Non-Verbal Cues

> "If you're not using your smile you're like a man with
> a million dollars in the bank and no checkbook."
> —Les Giblin

Did you know that people are born with the ability to smile? Infants smile when they recognize a friendly face. In fact, according to Frank McAndrews, a psychology professor at Knox College, children born blind are "preprogrammed" to smile under the same circumstances as people who can see even though they have never seen anybody smile!

As smiling is an unlearned automatic behavior, it then makes complete sense that it's actually easier for your face to smile than it is to frown. It takes approximately 26 facial muscles to smile and over 50 to frown. That makes smiling a far more natural facial expression than frowning. The problem is we allow the mundane activities of life to wipe that smile from our faces.

There are some things in life that are easier to return once they're given. A smile is one of those things. When you smile at someone there is a high likelihood that person will return your smile. Try an experiment the next time you're walking past people on the street or in a mall. Whenever your eyes naturally meet with a stranger's, immediately send the person a genuine smile and you'll see that in most cases they'll return the smile. This is powerful. It means that you will have placed them, at least temporarily, in a positive state of mind. Is there one other act so easily achieved that can have such a positive and powerful affect over another human being (a person who is in fact a stranger)? In addition, you've also placed yourself in a positive mental state. Many times when we give something we receive something in return, without even asking for it.

"You Ain't Nothing But A Hound Dog."—Elvis Presley

I'd like you to stand in front of a mirror and repeat these words in a monotone voice without moving or even blinking: "You ain't nothing but a hound dog." Now, how did that sound? "Ridiculous," you say? Makes no sense, a useless sentence? Elvis Presley didn't think so when he sang those words in a song entitled "Hound Dog." That song went to the number one spot in 1956. Now you have proof that it's not just what you say, but how you say it that matters! Interestingly, if you read the words to almost any contemporary pop hit without using voice inflection you'll find they lose much of their resonance. A few more examples include: the Rolling Stones, "Get Off My Cloud," with the lines "Hey, you, get off my cloud, don't hang around 'cause two's a crowd"; Peter Gabriel, "Sledgehammer," "I want to be your sledgehammer, why don't you call my name"; Survivor, "Eye of the Tiger," "It's the eye of the tiger, it's the thrill of the fight"; or Queen, "Radio Ga Ga" lyrics, "All we hear is radio ga ga, radio goo goo, radio ga ga." None make an emotional appeal unless they are delivered with appropriate vocal inflection. Why is that? Because there is great power in how we say what we say!

The same can be said for many great performers. They make the words come alive when they interpret a song through voice inflection. Think about how your favorite entertainers stir your emotions: comedians who make you laugh, actors who make you cry. The best put us in certain emotional states by using mere words. That is real power, and it is often rewarded with money and fame. Great entertainers know how to use their voices to make us laugh and cry. Often it's not what they say, but how they say it, that makes the difference. You don't have to be a professional entertainer to use this to your advantage. Do you approach every communication opportunity with the proper voice inflection in order to induce a certain mood?

Voice inflection is made up of three distinct parts: pitch, which represents the tone of a person's voice; rhythm, which is the pace or tempo of a person's pattern of speech; and volume, which obviously determines how loudly the person is communicating. Much can be learned from listening carefully to these three voice characteristics: Pitch, Rhythm and Volume.

Through my entrepreneurial endeavors I've been involved in literally hundreds of negotiations, meetings and interviews over the years. I've found that I can either be held mesmerized by what a person is saying or I can be unmoved, based not upon what the person might be saying, but how he or she is saying it. Those who are able to attach emotion to their voice through the proper use of pitch, rhythm and volume seem to be able to reach out and pull other people into their ideas.

I recall using such techniques when negotiating some of the early leases for one particular company. They were the usual types of negotiations, the landlord wanted quite a lot and I wanted to pay very little. My position was rather simple—I wanted to pay very little because that's what I had. Invariably, these negotiations came down to a final meeting that often took place on the telephone. I would convince my future landlord to see things my way and let me occupy the space for very little. How was I able to do this? I'm convinced that it was not totally because of what I said, but how I was saying it. What the landlord heard was a young entrepreneur speaking the truth about how his startup company could not afford to pay high rent. More importantly he heard me speak in almost hushed tones with broken rhythm as I described how difficult it was in the beginning. "I just can't afford . . . to pay what . . . you want." He also heard me raise my voice and show excitement and sincerity when I spoke about how faithfully we paid our landlords each month. "The check will be there before the first of every month. We've never missed paying our landlords early. It's money in the bank!" This was not an act; I was telling him the truth. More importantly, I was conveying the truth with proper voice inflection.

Aside from the finest actors and actresses who are able to move our emotions through the proper use of voice inflection, we have also witnessed some outstanding political communicators who have been similarly skilled, leaders who could communicate their feelings so well that you could feel their sincerity. Were they actually that sincere? Real or not, it was always difficult for me to turn away when they were speaking. I've already mentioned Ronald Reagan, who was referred to as "The Great Communicator" because he was able to convey, through voice inflection, what America wanted so badly to hear. Bill Clinton was also a powerful communicator. Clinton could turn the public opinion polls with a properly honed speech using expert voice inflection. I don't think it's a coincidence that they were both re-elected to a second term. Regardless of political affiliation, many people crossed party lines to vote for these men because each reached out and convinced the electorate to vote for them by tugging on their emotions through voice inflection.

Create The Mood, Don't Be Pulled Into A Bad One

Have you ever noticed that the angrier someone gets the louder they become? What do you usually do when the volume increases? Shout that person down, or run away? I've found through experience that the best thing to do when confronted by an angry, screaming individual is to speak in calm, quiet tones. This not only helps you to better collect your thoughts it also works psychologically to calm them as well. How does a mother comfort her crying baby? I think there is something in all of us that responds to calm comforting tones when we're angry. **If someone shouts at us and we meet that aggression with our own raised volume, we only escalate the temporary feud, usually causing hurt feelings and animosity.**

In the early days of my first large company our corporate office was located directly over one of the stores. One afternoon as I was working I couldn't help but overhear a customer loudly debating a point with our store manager. As I listened the discussion grew even more heated. Eventually it seemed that each person was attempting to shout down the other. At that point I opened my door and walked down the stairs and stood there. At this point the customer was enraged and when he saw me, he actually ran over to me and stopped just inches from my face and continued his angry rant. This was well within the eighteen-inch comfort zone usually allotted to those with whom you are communicating, and I was uncomfortable. But I stood my ground nonetheless, with my hands in front of me, the fingertips of one hand matching and touching the fingertips of the other.

I knew that if this person were violent he would have acted by now. He was, at this point, shouting directly in my face. He was close enough to me so that I could actually count the fillings in his teeth (not a pleasant moment). I remained calm until he was finished with his verbal assault. I then told him in a hushed voice that it was obvious that he was very angry, and I wanted to do everything in my power to turn him into a happy customer. He continued to shout at me, but something was missing, some of the steam had gone out of his delivery. His shouting had quieted down a notch or two. Then, when he was finished with this new tirade, I calmly informed him in the softest, most reassuring voice that I could muster, that whatever had occurred in the past could be rectified if he was interested. He continued to show his discontent, but this time the volume was just a little above normal. When he completed a few more sentences he just paused and looked at me. I could then begin to offer him some options, as he was now completely coherent and looking for answers. The problem was solved in less than five minutes. I didn't play into the heat of the moment. I created a different moment, and he played into that!

Never meet verbal aggression with verbal aggression if you want to solve a problem and have all parties walk away reasonably happy. In most cases the person is shouting because that's all he's capable of doing at the time due to his temporary emotional state. If he could, he would give you a list of reasons he's not happy. But he's been overtaken with emotion, and the end product is what you are hearing. Don't buy into his emotions by following him down that same heated path. Create your own avenue with a reasonable volume, accurate pitch, and rhythm, which will lead to better understanding, more cooperation, and ultimately a more satisfactory end result for all parties involved.

It doesn't matter what your True Vision might be, understanding how to communicate with someone who is verbally aggressive can help you.

"Oh what a tangled web we weave when first we practice to deceive."—Sir Walter Scott

It is unfortunate but as we head out into the world to make our True Vision a reality we will encounter people who stretch the truth to suit their own agenda. You might call them liars, because they are. You don't want their lies to stand in the way of your True Vision.

How do you spot a liar? Well, we know one thing for sure, you can't ask the person. Fortunately, I've found most people to be honest. However, there is that small minority that will attempt to deceive you. In the early days of building my first company, prior to forming a security team, I was in the unenviable position of occasionally having to question an employee about a missing deposit, a cash drawer that happened to come up short, or some other questionable activity. Invariably the guilty person would at first lie. Makes sense, they must have reasoned. Once you've committed a theft how important is a lie to cover it up? Lying can be very damaging; in fact it's as bad as stealing and it's far easier to successfully perform. It is also capable of covering up the thieves' other questionable activity.

His Mouth Said One Thing, His Body Said Another

In one particular case a manager complained that he was missing a $50 bill which had been sitting in his wallet on the counter when he went outside to assist a customer in front of the store. When he returned, the money was missing. The only other person in the store was his assistant manager.

At this point there were four possible explanations. The first and most obvious is that Tim, the assistant manager, removed the fifty when the manager stepped outside to assist the customer. Another explanation was that the manager, for some reason, was trying to set up his assistant manager to look like a thief and was falsely claiming that a $50 bill was removed. A third possibility was that the manager was mistaken regarding the amount he actually had in his wallet. The fourth possible scenario was that there was another person perhaps hiding in the store, who leaped out, rifled the wallet, removed the fifty, and then somehow made his escape with no one seeing him.

Well, which one was it? One of my colleagues at the corporate office stated flatly: "There is no way that Tim would steal $50 out of his own manager's wallet when in fact he was the only one in the store. It's just too obvious." I then went over the other possibilities with my colleague. If the manager wanted to set Tim up to look like a thief, he wouldn't need to use his own wallet to do so as there was a cash drawer with far more than $50 inside. Secondly, this particular manager was not prone to make financial errors, and when asked if he could have made a mistake, he was adamant that he had not. Finally, according to both people there was neither a customer nor an additional employee in the store; it was just the two of them. Do you realize yet what happened to the $50?

This was without a doubt the easiest case there has ever been. The assistant manager went into the manager's wallet and removed the $50. "He can't be guilty, it's just too obvious," my corporate office colleague commented. "Well, he is," I maintained.

When we questioned Tim he at first denied the theft as most thieves do. His body, speech, and mannerisms, however, told a different story. He immediately placed his hand over his mouth and subtly glanced away as he denied the charge. He continued to repeat many of these "tells" during the questioning. It was somewhat amusing to watch his body go through these completely incongruent motions as he was being questioned. While his mouth said one thing, his body said another. Finally, after only fifteen minutes of questioning (a very short time for this type of thing) Tim blurted out the truth. My colleague, who had a difficult time thinking that anyone would be so stupid as to remove $50 from a wallet when he would be the only suspect, was stunned. Occasionally, a thief will commit a crime that seems just too obvious for them to have performed in the hope of throwing you off the track. You may wrongly think, as my colleague did, that it was too obvious, and the guilty party could not have done it. There's one more possibility that I've found to be true through the years: in many cases thieves are just plain stupid!

Here's a short anecdote unrelated to communication errors but one that highlights the stupidity of thieves. One of my assistant managers from a former business actually shot himself in the arm, then took the money out of the cash drawer and walked it to his car. He then went back into the store and called the police, claiming that someone had just shot him and had taken the money. It only took a couple of minutes for the local police to track the blood trail from our store to the assistant manager's car. At this point the suspect had been nabbed, without much questioning needed. When you deal with thousands of employees over a period of years you learn that in most cases people who steal not only are dishonest, but also not very smart. Fortunately, they comprise a very small percentage of the workforce.

12 Reliable Signs You Are Being Lied To

Are you able to detect when a person isn't being honest with you? Here's a short list of what I have found to be some of the most obvious signs that a person is trying to mislead you (a more lengthy and comprehensive list is beyond the scope of this book):

1. **The person will bring a hand to his face.** This is a way for the liar to literally cover up his lie.

2. **Always look for a false smile that does not engage the eyes.** This is a deliberate attempt to ease you into your comfort zone so that the lie will be more quickly believed.

3. **Moving the head or body around in a nervous manner.** This can indicate that the liar is not yet comfortable with his own lie. This may stop, or slow down, after the liar has a chance to dig in and become better adjusted to the lie he's attempting to put over on you.

4. **Improper eye contact.** In this case the liar will either be looking away after his attempt to make you believe him, nervously looking everywhere but into your eyes, or, he may gaze a little too directly into your eyes in a strong attempt to get you to believe him. Either look is unnatural and suspicious.

5. **Facial tics.** These are usually a dead giveaway that the liar is uncomfortable with his own false premise. When this occurs the very statement that preceded the facial tic is in all likelihood a lie.

6. **A voice that is trailing off.** When someone begins to speak in a relatively normal volume and then starts trailing off, she is showing a lack of confidence in her own statement. In other words, the statement is even hard for her to believe.

7. **The liar will usually begin perspiring at some point upon questioning.** While anyone can become nervous and sweat a little when he is being questioned, a liar will immediately begin to sweat. He may even remark that it's the warmth of the room that's making him sweat. However, it's not the room that is too hot; it is the situation that he has gotten himself into.

8. **The pupils of the liar's eyes may become enlarged.** This is a more difficult signal to become aware of, as you have to be sitting relatively close to the liar to notice.

9. **Throat-clearing.** The person will clear his throat as it becomes more difficult for him to talk. I'm sure you've heard the term "choking under pressure." That term is based upon the fact that as a large degree of stress is thrust upon the liar, his vocal cords may begin to constrict which causes him to clear his throat, cough, or to actually choke.

10. **The untruthful person may either ask you to repeat a question, or take an unusual amount of time to answer your question.** This is an obvious attempt to make up something on the spot that's believable.

11. **Look out for the too-short answer, which carries with it no explanation or details.** The liar in this case wants to get in and out as painlessly as possible. There are no details given because he would have to make them up, which can be too difficult to do under questioning.

12. **A change in the details of the original story.** When this happens, the liar has forgotten the original lie, and is now inadvertently changing his story. While anyone can forget a tiny detail or two, the liar will leave out important pieces of the original story, or actually change certain parts of the original story. He's lost in his "tangled web of deception."

While it's possible that the person may show most or all of the above twelve "tells," in some cases you won't be quite so fortunate. Be aware, ready to read the person, and look for as many of these signals as they display.

In the story involving the missing $50 bill I had the advantage of knowing with a high degree of certainty that Tim was the guilty party before I ever asked one single question. However, being able to read another person in any situation, even one with high integrity, is extremely helpful. Pay attention to not only what a person is saying, but also how they say it, and what his body is doing while he says it. Keep a careful eye on the person, and mentally note certain mannerisms. And when possible establish baseline behavior (behavior that the person displays during normal conversation) prior to the actual encounter. For example: if someone always has a nervous facial tic, then obviously that's one mannerism that you would not necessarily attribute to lying.

Don't let anyone steal your True Vision with a lie! Always be aware of the other person's true intentions by memorizing the "tell" list above.

Communicating With The Proper Person

While how you say what you say is extremely important, it's just as important to make sure you say it to the right person.

Have you ever practiced meaningless chatter? You have, if you've done one of the following: complained to a co-worker regarding your working conditions, or talked endlessly to someone about how you plan on losing weight or stopping the cigarette habit. Have you talked to death the idea that one day you'll start a business and build a fortune?

It's obvious that desiring better working conditions, quitting smoking, losing weight and starting your own business are all worthy Visions. My questions to you are: Who are you saying them to, and what is the end result of your repeated communication to those people? If you are like some, you may be saying the wrong things to the wrong people on a regular basis. **While venting your emotions is a healthy thing to do, there is a difference between expressing your personal feelings and actually <u>doing</u> something productive about your circumstances.** If you have been practicing any of the unproductive actions listed above and you find yourself in the same undesirable situation year after year, then you've been practicing meaningless chatter.

Meaningless chatter can sometimes make us feel better by allowing us to vent our frustrations. But in the end all you come up with is a short-term gain for a long-term loss. In the examples above you have allowed meaningless chatter to take the place of more productive communication, which can help you reach your True Vision.

Once you have uncovered your True Vision, you will need to approach people who can assist you in making it a reality. It really doesn't matter what your True Vision may be; you'll still need to communicate appropriately with this person if you are to realize this Vision. No one fully succeeds in life on his own. If people accomplish something of significance it's not only because they had a True Vision for that particular thing, but also because they convinced enough people and have gotten their help and support. **The bigger the Vision, the more people you need to support it. The only way that you attract others to support your Vision is by Effective Communication.** As I've previously cautioned, don't waste your time communicating your Vision to the wrong people, or communicating it too early. If you do you'll most likely be either scorned or ignored. Your Vision may even be trampled so badly that you begin to believe that what you want most in life is unattainable. Once this feeling sets in, you may even want to quit. You don't need that!

When it's time to reach out to someone and share your Vision make sure that it is to the appropriate person. If your True Vision is to start your own business, then why are you sharing that with your unemployed neighbor? Your unemployed neighbor may be a very nice person and you might share some fun social times together, but what does this "nice person" know about starting a business? Has he ever been involved with running his own business? Does he know anyone personally who has run his own business? If the answer is no, stop wasting your time. Seek out someone who has done what you're eager to do yourself, someone who is living his or her own True Vision as an entrepreneur. Try to learn from that person's mistakes. Seek guidance and techniques from that person. Remember that just because you happen to be friends with someone doesn't make that person the best authority on helping you realize your Vision. You may have to be introduced to the best person to help you by someone who knows both of you. You may have to cultivate a relationship with a third party in order to even get close enough to have a discussion with the appropriate person. This may take a bit of networking and some time, but it will be well worth it.

On the other hand, depending on exactly what your True Vision is, it may be quite easy for you to find someone who has been where you're going. I think we all know at least one person who has successfully quit smoking. How did they do it? What worked for that person? How long did it take? What was the most difficult part? Would this person be willing to assist you in a "buddy program"? People who have been where you are understand the importance of a helping hand. It's your duty to find the proper person and ask these questions. You might be able to model their successful behavior in achieving your True Vision.

Maybe it's money that you need to realize your True Vision of becoming an entrepreneur and you are looking for investors. You need to let the person who could help you know exactly when he will get his money back, and how much he will make from the deal. In other words you have to be ready to answer "what's in it for them." People are usually motivated by self-interest, so be sure they understand how they will benefit through their involvement in your business deal. Be precise in your communication. Make sure you don't wander from the point. The person you are approaching for money, whether he is a banker or a friend or a relative with extra cash, needs to completely understand why you need the money, and when it will be returned with a profit. He or she will not be interested in flamboyant plans and colorful dreams of where you would like to be someday. A banker is interested in the safe return of the bank's capital with a profit, period! Far too many times a potential financial investor is scared away by someone who is not communicating properly at the start.

How I Learned By Failing "Communication 101"

I remember one particular day early in the growth of my first large company. I was in my office with a local banker who liked my company's financial numbers, and the meeting was going well. "You have really built a good company here with a very healthy bottom line. I don't see any reason why we can't stand behind you for some funds," he said while nodding his head and smiling approvingly. I had only a handful of stores at the time and at this point, it seemed like I was assured I would get the money I needed to go forward with the next phase of my expansion. Then it happened! Pushing back a sliding door on the wall I revealed a huge map of the United States. On this map were colored pins, each representing either a current competitor, a future competitor, one of my current stores or a location for a future store. This was a great visual for exactly what I wanted to ultimately accomplish. The problem was that it was not such a good visual for a conservative banker who only foresaw an additional two stores in the immediate future.

Now I knew that I was not going to be foolhardy and open hundreds of stores overnight, but the banker had a different view: "Now don't get carried away, if you grow too fast you can lose everything," he said as he stood up and folded his arms in front of him. The banker continued on, "There was someone not long ago who began a tractor company and tried to expand too quickly and now he's bankrupt." His eyebrows furrowed with concern. I saw immediately the mistake that I'd made. It was too late, however; it was like standing on the tracks in front of a freight train as it picked up speed. I started to say, "No, I am quite careful regarding . . ." but he interrupted me (this man could not be stopped), "The problem is not always with you, the economy could take a turn for the worse, or there could be other tragic events where we have no control," he said. I tried interjecting one last time: "This is just what I want to do eventually if everything goes according to plan." He wouldn't hear of it. By then it was too late, he wasn't listening and I had lost him. His body language went from warm and friendly to cold and hostile. His demeanor had already told me what I needed to know. I received a rejection letter several weeks later, turning down my request for a loan. I was upset but determined to learn from my communication error.

I failed Communication 101 that day. Never ever paint an aggressive, grandiose picture of what you want to do someday in front of a conservative banker. You explain why the next couple of stores will work, and then leave it at that until the time comes for further expansion. Had I done so, by then he may have gotten used to the way I worked and achieved a certain comfort level based on my track record. Every rule has an exception. I eventually met the right banker for my plans and grew the company to 250 stores. Not all bankers make such conservative judgements; most are thoughtful and obviously trying to be mindful of how the bank's money is invested. To an eager entrepreneur, however, this can be a very tedious, all consuming process, which never seems to end. But it was a necessary part of making my True Vision come true.

Be Specific, Be Complete

When the time is right and once the proper people are found to communicate with, make sure that you communicate specifically, and thoroughly. Do you need a loan to begin a business? Let them know exactly how much you need for that specific project by designing a complete business plan. This may seem obvious, but it's been my experience that people sometimes ask for too little to fund their project and in addition put forth an ineffective business plan. The problem usually is that the amount and structure are not clear in your own mind, so therefore they cannot be properly articulated. A good business plan should be done well in advance of meetings with possible financiers.

For example, if you're in need of two hundred thousand dollars in order to launch your entrepreneurial venture, then *ask* for at least that much, but provide a specific breakdown as to where every penny is going. There is nothing more discouraging than to be shot down because your potential financier does not understand what the money is for, or why it is so important. This requirement to be precise extends to any Vision you might have. If your True Vision is weight loss, it's important to be precise when communicating with your spouse so he or she knows how much weight you plan to lose and exactly how he or she can help you achieve this Vision. How many of you have tried to lose weight only to have your spouse inadvertently work against you? "Let's just slide through this fast food burger joint, honey." But . . . but . . . too late! **All the important people in your life must be on board with you, or it becomes more difficult to succeed!**

Most successful people are good communicators, which helps them become successful in many things. As you become a good communicator you'll be better able to explain your point of view to those who can help you achieve your True Vision!

But how can you become a better communicator? By learning from your mistakes. Below is a list of communication taboos. Are you guilty of any of these mistakes? If so, this could be the reason you have not yet achieved your True Vision.

7 Major Communication Errors

1. **Stop Whining**. Not getting what you want? Fine, change your approach, but don't expect people to listen to you whine about your problems. Asking for something in a whiney tone of voice is just annoying.

   If you think about it, you are not entitled to anything, except life, liberty, and the pursuit of happiness. When you whine you're saying in essence that you are entitled to the very thing that you are whining about. It also conveys a certain immaturity and negativity, as immature negative people always feel like life owes them something (some teens tend to do this). So drop the whine and the entitlement mentality, speak out like a thinking, intelligent adult who is ready to work hard and smart for what you want.

2. **Don't Interrupt.** This may seem obvious but you would be amazed by the number of people who can't hold their tongues an extra few seconds to let the person they are talking with finish his thought. When you interrupt you are not validating what the other person is saying. In fact, what you are saying is, "I have something more important to say so be quiet." If you have an important thought and you don't want to lose it, bring along a paper and pen, and write it down. This way not only are you avoiding the interruption mistake, but it looks as if you're taking notes about what the other person is saying. This would be considered a high compliment indeed.

3. **Repeating Yourself Endlessly.** Repeating yourself once, or maybe even twice, in certain situations is a good way to make sure that your thought has been properly transferred. The problem is that sometimes when you're discussing an issue that is important to you, you may have a tendency to over-emphasize it by repeating your main point several times. When this occurs you're inadvertently telling the other person that you think they are slow or not intelligent enough so you must continue to repeat yourself. You're also signaling that their needs are not important, you're just after your own wants and desires and continue to push them until you get what you want.

4. **Getting Off the Subject.** When you're asking for a favor or guidance from someone, make sure that you stay on the subject. When you drift and begin to ramble, you not only take up a great deal of the other person's time, but you make yourself appear unfocused and poorly prepared. If you have a common interest, naturally you can spend some time discussing it. Make sure, however, that you circle back to the purpose of exactly why you are there. Respect the other person by using your meeting time wisely.

5. **Do Not Demean Yourself Or Others.** Have you ever tried to endear yourself to others by demeaning yourself? "I'm always late too." "I would forget my head if it were not attached." "I have a hair-trigger temper, what can I say?" While this may be

accepted when you're among friends, it's a career crusher and business stopper when you're dealing with professionals. The person whom you are attempting to persuade will only be put off by your inappropriate confessions. If a person wants to demean himself in your presence, by all means let them. He may feel so comfortable around you that it slips out. This could be a credit to your ability to make another person feel comfortable. It's more likely, however, he or she is interested in getting you to discuss your shortcomings.

On a similar note when you put other people down you simultaneously put yourself down as well. Don't be baited into a conversation about someone else's abilities. As soon as you attack someone who is not there to defend himself, you look cheap and petty in the other person's view. Oh, I know it may feel good to talk about someone that you may not like, but it's a bad idea. Whether you're just chatting as a faceless, nameless entity on the Internet, or you are in a professional or social setting, gossiping and rumor mongering are cowardly acts that will bring you neither respect nor higher esteem in the other person's mind.

6. **Don't Assume**. You may have heard this adage before: "When you assume, you make an 'ass' out of 'u' and 'me'." I have no idea where that statement originated, but it's as true today as it was when I first heard it. Please don't leave any important meeting not fully understanding what was discussed. Know what your next move should be, and make sure that the other person is aware that you understand his, or her, position on the subject. **Good communication doesn't always result in agreement. It should, however, result in complete understanding.** A brief summary may be in order if you're not clear about a particular detail. It's far better to mention it and ask for clarification prior to the meeting's end than to leave, be unclear, and suffer the consequences later. If you're embarrassed to ask about something, simply lump it in with items that you are clear on in summary fashion. If you wedge it between two points that you're quite clear on, you'll feel more comfortable while mentioning it.

7. **Negative Body Language**. I mentioned body language earlier, but you not only need to read other people's body language, you need to project proper body language yourself. As we know,

nonverbal communication can sometimes send stronger messages than the spoken word. Make sure that when you're in a serious discussion you make proper eye contact. Don't shift your gaze in an impatient manner. Also, when seated, lean forward and scoot a bit more toward the end of your chair. This will indicate enthusiasm and interest on your part. Never cross your arms in front of you as that subconsciously puts people off. If you're at a table, simply fold your hands in front of you, or just keep them on the table near each other. Don't place your hands below the table; this makes your shoulders slump forward and gives you a hunched appearance. Never cover any part of your face with your hands either. You want the other person to see all of your facial expressions, as they will hopefully help convey the proper message.

Good communication skills can be learned and developed. Be alert to what you are attempting to convey, choose your words carefully, and above all make sure that you have not been misunderstood or that you have not misunderstood the other person. And certainly always be respectful, especially when you don't feel like it. Our lives revolve around different types of people, each with his or her own agenda. By communicating properly you will be able to build relationships with those who can help you achieve your True Vision. Before you move on to the next section of the book, use the Urgency Factor right now by writing down your biggest communication errors. This will help you become aware of specific areas that may need improvement.

chapter nine

VISION STEP: CREATING POSITIVE ACCURATE PERCEPTIONS

We don't see things as they are;
we see things as we are.
　　—Anais Nin

Your perception of the world becomes your reality, whether or not that perception is correct. Your perception of the real world is also very personal. It's based on events that have taken place in your life, and other views you've adopted as your own based on things you've seen, books and articles you've read, and people that you've listened to. Many variables can determine your perception of the world around you and how you perceive your chances of success in that world.

How The Media Colors Your Perception Of Reality

Because perception is indeed so very personal, we sometimes are too sensitive to things that should be regarded more generally. For instance, whenever the news media reports on employment statistics, it never tells you how many Americans in the workforce are gainfully employed. What they do tell you is that unemployment, for example, has risen to 10%. Upon hearing this you feel a certain unrest: things seem to be falling apart, you tell yourself; unemployment is now double digits and we must be doomed! If you are unemployed, you immediately feel there is no hope for you. How can there be any hope when unemployment has risen to 10%. What horror!

Hold on now; let's look at this with a Positive Accurate Perception. If unemployment is 10% that also means that a full 90% of the workforce is employed! Unless you view yourself (perception again) as being in the very bottom of the workforce, in dead last place, things are not all that bad. According to recent information from the U.S. Bureau of Labor Statistics, there are just under 140 million people employed in the USA. Do you perceive that every single one of the 140 million people are more employable than you? Keep in mind you're only looking for one job, not 140 million jobs, just one job in order to improve your life. Let me remind you, you're not a statistic. You're a human being with a set of very unique skills and abilities which, when pointed in the right direction and assisted with the proper amount of Vision, can get you just about any job you want! Have you ever perceived it like that before? It really is all about perception, and yours is about to get much better with a True Vision that will help you every step of the way. Let's further examine the media's role in limiting your thinking and unwittingly attempting to replace that positive running movie in your mind's eye with a negative one.

Each day the media gives us all sorts of negative imagery: accidents, poverty, natural disasters, man-made disasters, financial ruin, human suffering, and death. The question you must ask yourself repeatedly: is this an accurate representation of your world? Does it totally reflect reality? Or is it in fact a very small portion of reality, mixed with sensational headlines in order to help sell more news to the public?

Repetition has a very powerful influence on that constantly running movie that plays in the theater of your mind (one reason why Affirmation Reminders are powerful). Repeated viewing of negative imagery will plant that image firmly before your mind's eye, replacing a potentially productive mental movie with a harmful one. Even if the imagery is not being accurately represented it will still distort your perception. Repeated on a daily basis it will become accepted as fact, even though it's only a very small part of the total picture. For example, according to the Department of Justice, violent crimes in general, the homicides, burglaries, property crime, and a host of other crimes, are all down significantly over the past 15 years. Yet, I'd wager that if you took a random survey of passers-by the overwhelming majority would swear that crime rates are worse than ever.

The same can be said for major diseases. According to the American Cancer Society and the US Centers for Disease Control and Prevention, cancer deaths are down for the majority of various cancers. The American Heart Association also states that the annual death rate from coronary heart disease has dropped dramatically over the past 15 years! Where are all the reports on the good news? Don't hold your breath waiting, or you'll pass out and wind up as just another negative statistic. Most news outlets would have you believe that every businessperson is crooked, every politician is corrupt, and every athlete is on some kind of performance enhancing drug. Even though these bad apples represent only a tiny portion of each group, you are still left with the impression that just about every public figure is involved in some sort of reprehensible activity, thanks to the mainstream media!

I'm certainly not claiming that there isn't bad news, obviously there is. However, many things are actually much better than they were over a decade ago. What *has* drastically changed is the speed in which we hear the news and the many sources that are now available to report on it. Compared to several years ago we now have literally hundreds of television channels, satellite radio, the Internet, and a plethora of magazines and books, bringing us the latest in what? Bad news! Perhaps the news in some areas has worsened some, but hearing and reading it repeatedly magnifies the intensity, and to what end? In fact, if we allow it, it can give us a feeling of hopelessness and despair.

The answer is not to bury your head in the sand and pretend that the world is perfect. On the contrary I feel that you should be aware of what is happening in your world. The answer lies in managing how much of this negatively spun information you allow yourself on a daily basis. Does it help or hurt your perception to take in a steady diet of negative news from a multitude of sources each day? I think we know the answer to that. Anything that warps your perception and changes that ever-playing mental movie to negative in some way harms your chances of success. However, it's certainly not just the media that has the power to distort your perception of your world. As we shall see next, you can also do it to yourself if you're not careful.

One-Sided Perception

Here are three scenarios that may, or may not, sound familiar, but they are good examples of what I call one-sided perception.

You heard about a great restaurant that you've wanted to try, so you and your spouse stop in to see if it's as good as everyone says. The waitress walks up to your table, plops down two glasses of water and some of it spills on the table. She practically tosses two menus at you, then turns on her heels without even a smile, and walks away. (By the way, the point of this story is not about her poor communication skills.) Several thoughts rush to mind: "no tip for her" or "this is the last time I eat here." If you're mad enough you might even get up and walk out.

You're driving down the street, and someone cuts you off while exceeding the speed limit by at least 20 miles per hour. They begin behind you, dart out of their lane, pass you, abruptly cut in front of you, and then just as quickly, they turn left at the next intersection. You lay on your horn and start hollering at the driver, as if he can actually hear you. Red faced and upset, you drive on.

Finally, you're walking down the street and see a good friend coming your way. You smile, tip your head back and begin to raise your hand to say hello. Then suddenly, just as you stop to talk, she looks the other way and keeps walking. In fact, on second thought, you begin to believe that she picked up her speed as she walked past. You're immediate reaction? "How dare she snub me! After all I've done for her; she looked right at me too!"

I'm sure you realize that there are extenuating circumstances in each of these scenarios that might otherwise alter your perception. In the first story, the waitress's mother just died and she had used all of her time off. She had to go to work or lose her job (she doesn't work for kind understanding people). In the second scenario the driver was taking his wife to the hospital because of emergency complications from her pregnancy. And in the final story, your friend just lost her job and was walking down the street in a daze. She really didn't see you, or much of anything else.

It's easy to fall into the habit of having a one-sided perception when you only have one side of the facts. The wiser and more difficult thing to do is to wait until you do have all the facts, so that you have a true multi-sided view of the other person's reality, or, in the case of the examples above, you see each situation for what it really is. Since, in those instances, there is no way of seeing every side from the angle that you were at, the prudent thing to do is not form an immediate one-sided perception (some call this giving a person the benefit of the doubt). When we only perceive part of a situation it's easy to walk away with a distorted perception of reality. Sometimes how we perceive a situation touches even closer to home, which can leave us with a distorted view of how things really work.

It Happened To Me Therefore It Happens To Everyone

Have you ever been involved in a situation that impacted you so greatly that it changed the way you perceived reality? Perception can be distorted by a first-hand event that takes place during a time in your life when you are most vulnerable. For example, both you and your brother-in-law are unemployed at the same time. Your brother-in-law finds a job because he has a friendship with someone at a certain company. From that point forward you might think that knowing someone inside a company is the only way to get a good job. You perceive this as fact because this was a very personal event in your life, and it touched you deeply. You and your brother-in-law both needed a job. Your brother-in-law obtained a job because of someone he knows, and you're still unemployed. It doesn't get much more personal than that, does it? Events like this tend to distort your perception of reality every time they happen.

What you have to remember with the above example is that the majority of evidence does not lineup with your perception of how people become gainfully employed. People apply for jobs all the time. While it always helps to have someone at a company who can speak for you, it usually doesn't happen that way. Out of the almost 140 million employed workers in America how many do you think actually knew someone at the company where they work before they were hired? There's certainly no way to tell, but I would wager that the figure would probably be under 1% of the total. However, for the sake of our example, let's say that the figure is an incredibly high 5% of the total! If that's the case, that means that while 7 million people were fortunate enough to get a job because they knew someone within the company, a full 133 million people obtained employment without the assistance of an insider. Even if we doubled that outrageously high figure, that would still only be 10% of the workforce. That would mean that 126 million people became gainfully employed based on their own merits!

What may have worked for your brother-in-law is not necessarily what takes place, to a large degree, in the real world. It's certainly not the reality of the overwhelming majority of our workforce, who found their employment the old-fashioned way, on their own. If your True Vision is of a new career there's no reason you can't do the very same thing, and even do it better and faster!

Try not to allow your Positive Accurate Perception to be distorted by personal events that take place in your life. This can tend to keep you from achieving, rather than help you to achieve, your True Vision. Keep in mind it may take only one incident to cloud the lens of perception. From this point forward you may carry with you a long-term distorted perception which will only harm you. Let's look further at how a Positive Accurate Perception can be changed to a distorted perception fairly easily.

Don't Play The Grudge Game

Have you ever perceived a slight from someone and you're still carrying a grudge? Maybe the perceived slight came from a neighbor, friend, or a co-worker. Some people actually hold grudges against entire companies because one person waiting on them one time may have had a bad day and was rude. I know one person who refuses to go back to a certain restaurant because on the day that she chose to visit, it was busy, and she wasn't seated fast enough. A grudge is a feeling of resentment strong enough to seek revenge. In fact, when you ignore that person or entity this becomes your way of taking revenge, by "punishing" them for the perceived slight. You are taking away your conversation, your attention, or your business and hoping that you will cause them to feel badly. All of this is very negative, and helps no one. It also keeps you living in the past as you replay that person's perceived slight over and over in the theater of your mind. Most of us have fallen prey to this negative nonsense at one time or another.

The most important question becomes, how is continuing to perceive that person as an enemy and replaying that negative mental movie helping you? Truthfully, doing so actually punishes you! Think of it another way. If someone could somehow force you to think of a negative situation repeatedly, you would be upset with him or her, as that would punish you. But that is exactly what you are willingly doing to yourself. Certainly the situation which caused you to first perceive that slight is not worth the negative mental energy that it takes to carry it on for any length of time. I've been on both sides of a grudge before. Early on I was emotional enough to hold one, and have been the target of them as well. One day it dawned on me that ignoring the person and rerunning that negative mental movie repeatedly were only hurting me. This is also backed up by science. Researchers at the Harvard Medical School have found that nursing a grudge can put your body through the same strains as major stressful events, causing similar increases in muscle tension, blood pressure, and sweating. Further studies have shown links for reductions in heart rate, blood pressure, and overall workload for the heart when one is forgiving a betrayal.

If a person wants to hold a grudge against you that is his or her choice. I know the type some live off their hate; so that it becomes part of who they are. Little do they know that it will take a real physical and mental toll on them, even if they don't think so. But don't you play the grudge game: forgive, and move on. Forgiveness is like any other skill, the more you do it the better you will get at it. Make sense? If you don't want that person in your life, that's another matter. Move on, but leave the grudge behind because that only hurts you. More importantly, it cannot help you in achieving your True Vision, but it certainly could hurt. Carrying a grudge is heavy lifting, and your mental energy—all of it—needs to be conserved and focused on the thing that matters most, your True Vision. You actually win the grudge game by not playing!

More Distorted Perceptions Which Could Harm Your True Vision

When we get a certain idea in our heads, we all tend to cling stubbornly to it, even if it has little basis in fact. This sort of tenacity is not a good thing as it will likely distract you and cloud your thinking, which can sabotage your True Vision. Let's take a look at a few more distorted perceptions and then the accurate response, which is the Positive Accurate Perception:

1. **Distorted Perception:** My uncle started a business and went broke, so even though I always wanted to own my own business, I think I'll forget about it.

   Positive Accurate Perception: While it's not easy to operate your own small business, it can be very lucrative, and well worth the effort. According to the U.S. Senate Committee on Small Business and Entrepreneurship, there are 27 million small businesses operating in the United States. They actually create two-thirds of all new jobs on a yearly basis. And according to a recent survey by *Salary.com*, the national average salary for a small business owner is $258,400 per year. If you make more (or less) than that, and are perfectly happy with what you're doing, then by all means keep doing it. However, if you'd like to look through the lens of a Positive Accurate Perception, use your uncle's experience as a learning tool. Find out what he did wrong, and learn from his mistakes. You can try a different approach using his loss as your gain. Reconsider the possibility of starting your own small business. Sure there's always the possibility that you'll go broke, just like your uncle did. But there's also a possibility that you'll become the first millionaire in your family! What is your True Vision?

2. **Distorted Perception**: All those business executives on Wall Street are thieves and liars.

Positive Accurate Perception: There are some thieves on Wall Street and when they steal it makes headlines because it's large, and we know that the press loves negative headlines. Just one high level thief who has access to a large company coffer can steal millions before being caught and prosecuted. At the same time, we don't usually read about the convenience store clerk who steals $5 or $10 each day. She usually doesn't make news, she just gets fired and the incident is forgotten. In fact, according to the 2006 National Retail Security Survey, almost 50% of all business loss is not from customers who shoplift, but from employee theft. Shoplifters account for just over 30% of all retail losses. An Ernst & Young study found that "retailers lose about $46 billion annually to inventory shrinkage, which is mostly employee theft." I'm sure you'll agree that is a shocking number. The point is stealing is wrong at every level but when is the last time you saw a headline which reported the billions lost in employee theft? It is just not as sensational a headline, is it?

Whether the theft originates on Wall Street or Main Street, human nature, which includes temptation, is the real culprit. The income level that a person attains does not make him either honest or dishonest. Personally, I would have less patience with someone who is entrusted with more and then betrayed that trust. If you are entrusted with more, more is expected of you. However, regardless of the income level of the thief, stealing is wrong. Other than that, the difference is that the executive made headlines, and the clerk got fired and just walked away.

3. **Distorted Perception:** Lottery winners are so lucky. If I came into some big money I'd be the happiest person in the world!

Positive Accurate Perception: We all think that winning a large sum of lottery money would add greatly to our happiness, and in the short-term it does. But studies of and interviews with people who received large unexpected financial windfalls such as winning the lottery, or collecting a large inheritance, reveal a surprisingly darker long-term picture. **It seems that cultivating a True Vision for wealth and succeeding on your own merits is inherently more emotionally healthy than striking it rich the easy way.**

One thing we need to understand is that human happiness is far more complicated than we think. While individual levels will vary, approximately half of our happiness is based on genetics. This is called a "happiness set-point." The good news is that we can control the other half. There are many things that you can do to raise your set-point and I will address that in the next chapter. For now, I want to focus your attention on the distorted perception that instant money can bring long-term happiness. The fact is the reverse may very well be true!

Two researchers, Philip Brickman and Donald Campbell, concluded in a landmark study just how important set-points are, and how our behavior and psychological responses flow from that, no matter how much our circumstances may abruptly change. In short, they found what they called a "hedonistic treadmill." Money does not buy happiness, and the pursuit of it in an attempt to gain happiness is futile. While winning money may give you temporary happiness, you eventually end up back at your set-point, where you began.

The primary reason for this, they explain, is that humans quickly adapt to their current situation, regardless of the new material object that may have added to their short-term happiness. People habituate regardless, whether that situation is good or bad. In other words, if you have the money to purchase a new car, that new car will give you immediate happiness. However, as you adjust to your new car your happiness will, in a relatively short period of time, go back to a certain set-point where it began. The new car that you raved about to your friends (some were even happy for you) becomes just a means of transportation after so many days or weeks. If you have plenty of sudden cash, and once again need to boost that happiness and have that same great feeling as you did when you first purchased your new car, you may then buy a new house. This raises your level of happiness once again, but only for a short period of time, until you adjust to your new circumstances and your level of happiness goes back to your original set-point. The hedonistic treadmill continues to spin in the false expectation that your sudden big windfall can buy you happiness.

One reason that lottery winners are, for the most part, not as happy as they expected to be is that after the hills and valleys of their buying binge are over, they too return to their natural happiness set-point, back where it was prior to their large influx of cash. But some are actually less happy than they were prior to winning the money. This is due largely to the constant letdown of placing so much emphasis on material objects, which only temporarily boost their happiness. And that's if they are fortunate! Some lottery winners end up far worse off than they were.

When Money *Didn't* Buy Happiness

Case #1: William "Bud" Post won 16.2 million dollars in a 1988 Pennsylvania lottery. He eventually commented, "I wish it never happened. It was totally a nightmare." Part of Post's unhappiness: In just one lawsuit filed against him (there were others), a girlfriend successfully sued for part of his windfall. A family member was arrested because he allegedly hired a hit man to kill Post. Could he have been hoping for a quick inheritance? After nonstop pestering from relatives, Post invested in not one but two losing business propositions. He was arrested for firing a gun over the head of a bill collector. All of this stress may have been a contributing factor to the heart problems he developed that consequently required an operation. Finally, Post declared bankruptcy, and today lives partially on government assistance.

Case #2: Evelyn Adams was "lucky" enough to twice win the New Jersey state lottery. Her jackpots totaled 5.4 million dollars. According to a recent published report, the money is completely gone due to gambling and because of relatives who just had to have a loan but might have forgotten to pay it back.

Case #3: A machinist before he won 1 million dollars in the Michigan state lottery, a now wealthy Ken Proxmire moved to California and went into business with family members (often not a good idea by the way). Approximately five years later he was bankrupt. One can only imagine the pain that he suffered when he went broke, taking several family members with him. Can there be any question that they blamed him? He is currently back at his former job as a machinist, quite a bit poorer, but I bet much wiser and happier.

Case #4: Missourian Janite Lee won a whopping 18 million dollars in 1993! According to reports she was very generous, and gave away significant amounts of her unearned cash to political causes, colleges, friends, and her community. In addition to that, she fell into the usual trap of chasing happiness by purchasing a million-dollar house, several cars, and other material trappings. All of that and she was a gambler too! According to published reports she filed for bankruptcy in 2001. Apparently she was left with only $700.

There are many more similar stories of those who received large amounts of money through the lottery or by way of unexpected inheritance. To be fair, many do end up well, but there are usually unique circumstances behind these outcomes (which I will cover later). Overall, the entire picture is disappointing relative to expectations. Why does it seem to end so tragically for so many instant money winners? Even those whose lives are not turned upside down still do not find the happiness they thought would follow their huge windfall. That is because the hedonistic treadmill acts as a powerful deception. Let's take a quick look at the many traps which are set for those who think fast wealth also means instant happiness.

1. **Money, like other powerful tools, takes a skilled hand to manage.** Most people who win large sums of money do not have that skill, and apparently do not even try to acquire it after they become rich. They assume that they were unhappy to begin with because they did not have enough money, and then illogically assume that having it now will make them happier. Now if you were actually destitute and living in the street, this might be true; however, when it comes to finances, most people are unhappy because they never had the ability to manage the money

they already had and racked up debt that was unsustainable. When they have a large influx of cash they automatically assume that they are now in good financial shape. Unfortunately, many end up mismanaging the large amount just as they did the smaller amount. The only difference is that the bills are larger. The end result is the same. Those who hire professional financial advisors to manage their money should make sure they are hiring someone who is experienced and trustworthy, and someone they know will look upon them as an important client. Without those three qualities there will be trouble ahead!

2. **Family, friends, and even some strangers who want to be your friend really want you to "invest" in their great idea.** At first you'll politely decline because you're a prudent individual. Then, out of the blue, certain pressures will be brought to bear on you by Mom, or dear Aunt Kate who really feels that you should partner with Cousin Jason, or at least loan him some money. After all, you have so much, and he has so little. Of course if you have no relatives or friends, you're safe.

3. **The jealousy factor also plays a role.** "She didn't earn that money and doesn't deserve it." You, too, may have that uneasy feeling in the back of your mind that you did not earn your bonanza. I think this is part of what causes lottery winners to give so much away so freely. And when you give a loan or gift to this one, how can you not do it for that one, and pretty soon there is a line forming around the block. You're a good guy right? You don't want people to think badly of you, and after all you were there once and know how it feels to be in need. Insecurity, the feeling that you didn't quite deserve your good fortune, misdirected empathy, and goodwill drive you to do things you shouldn't. And you go from being the richest and most popular guy around to the poorest and least popular. It's funny how that works.

4. **When you win a large amount of money, you automatically quit your job.** Why not quit? You don't need the income and you really don't like getting out of bed early every day to go to that nasty old job, so why not quit? Unfortunately, this removes something important in your life that you may not even know

you need, called structure. Many don't feel they need that kind of structure, because they can occupy their time fishing, jogging, skydiving, hiking, visiting friends, traveling, or any number of things that they enjoy or have always wanted to do. They wrongly assume that this is how they will get their structure. The problem is, it just doesn't work that way. Structure is the result of commitment and obligation; it's something that you *have* to do, something you may not want to do at the time but know is good for you in the long-term. Why is structure so important? Without structure you drift. Drifting is okay for a short period of time; it is called taking a vacation. Beyond that it's called the beginning of ruin. When there is no structure there is a constant void that needs to be filled. Some try to fill it with material possessions, others by constant partying, still others find even more creative ways to occupy themselves, but usually it all ends the same way, badly. Note some of the celebrities who struck it rich quickly or, worse yet, those who inherited a fortune. Happiness did not come attached to the money, because structure was not part of the deal!

5. **Overindulgence.** When people have all the money that they will ever need, quickly and without earning it, they sometimes think that also means they can have just about anything that they want. Unfortunately, if they are prone to overindulging at the dinner table, you can imagine what will happen with all the money and time they could ever want. If the big money winner is 20 pounds overweight right now, it won't be long before he or she is at least 60 or 70 pounds overweight.

It continues: if the windfall winner likes to drink a little too much, he may now be drinking most of the time because he has all the money and time that he needs. The restraints and the structure (that word again) are gone. If someone has a tiny lazy streak, guess who won't get out of bed some days? What if they have an eye for the opposite sex? They have the money and time to gravitate toward anything that pleases them. Unfortunately, every single one of their worst habits and desires will be magnified. With all restraints removed, there is nothing stopping them!

6. **You cannot buy self-discipline.** Another reason why fast money does not bring happiness is that in order to be able to manage such large sums of unexpected cash you need a superman-sized

dose of self-discipline. This is something that many people who slowly earn their way to the financial top may automatically understand. If you have earned and invested $25,000 productively, and then $50,000 and $100,000 with positive results, you have increased your ability to exercise Positive Self-Discipline, and also your money management skills. To the suddenly rich, every fiber in their being is screaming "spend it, spend it now!" Even if the person had a great deal of self-discipline before, he or she will still be tested. And if the person had none before, personal destruction will likely follow before long!

Fortunately The Odds Are Against You

One more fact to think about: consider that the odds of winning a state lottery can range anywhere from 8 million to 1 to 18 million to 1. Sometimes it's even greater depending on the size of the jackpot. The question is, does it really matter when the odds even get close to 1 million to 1? For example, depending on where you live, you have roughly a 1 in 500,000 chance of being struck by lightning this year. Does that put the chances of winning the lottery in better perspective? The states look at the lottery system as a voluntary tax, and if you are a participant, you are voluntarily giving up your hard-earned money to the state. That may be a smart revenue-enhancing move by the states, but not as smart a move by those participating. In many cases they are the very people who can least afford it.

I've spent the last several pages giving you a Positive Accurate Perception about going after fast money so that you will not invest your thinking on this distorted perception. Someday planning to win the lottery is not only foolhardy, but also diverts your attention away from a real possible means to financial independence. Rather, if you have a desire for riches, then develop a True Vision for obtaining wealth through your own abilities! What if you had invested every penny you had ever spent on a lottery ticket? How much would you be worth today?

You will gain far more than money on your way to success by earning it the old-fashioned way. You will develop the tools to manage it, the self-discipline to control it, and the self-esteem gained by climbing the ladder. You may also be able to raise that happiness set-point along the way. There will be more on happiness, and how to put yourself in the Glad Frame of Mind, in the next chapter. Now let's take a look at how a negative self-fulfilling prophecy can effect your perception to the point where you actually make the outcome worse!

Self-fulfilling Prophecy

As we saw in Chapter Eight, we can unknowingly create a self-fulfilling prophecy, which changes our perception of reality into something that can be quite negative and defeat our attempt to succeed. A negative self-fulfilling prophecy can affect your perception so that you are actually working against yourself! When wanting to be correct about your negative perception, you begin to act as if the worst were already happening, which in turn helps make that poor outcome a reality.

How you perceive a potential final result can either help or harm that outcome. You may have a negative self-fulfilling prophecy about your ability to get a job, start a business, lose weight, get out of debt, or a host of other worthy potential accomplishments. **When you have a negative self-fulfilling prophecy, you think and act both consciously and subconsciously to create the very thing that you do not want!** Because you do not want to defeat yourself in your attempt to achieve your True Vision, any negative self-fulfilling prophecies must be first discovered and then eliminated for the bad influences that they are!

For example, if a married woman has a false perception that her spouse is cheating, or will eventually cheat on her, she may do and say things that will ultimately drive him away and cause him to cheat. She might be overly concerned when he is not home on time and accuse him of cheating on her as soon as he comes in the door. She might imagine all sorts of things that are not really there—the scent of another woman's perfume, or a look that her husband never really gave that attractive woman at a party they attended. Negative self-fulfilling prophecies can lead to potentially terrible outcomes in every area of your life, in this case possibly irreparably damaging the couple's marriage.

The ultimate outcome of having a True Vision is actually the opposite of a negative self-fulfilling prophecy, isn't it? When we have a negative self-fulfilling prophecy we know in our hearts that the outcome is not going to be good. Oddly enough however, because we have predicted it, we sabotage ourselves both at a conscious and subconscious level to make sure that we are correct. When we have a True Vision we are both consciously and subconsciously focused on a positive outcome. Our perception of this future event is so very real and compelling that we do everything we can, at every level, to make it into a reality! Having a True Vision is a clearly positive choice, the other one is negative, but either is able to steer you toward a different life. Which one will you choose? The answer is to develop a True Vision that will ultimately create a life that becomes all you want it to be. Don't you agree? Next, I want to introduce you to what happens when we have a Positive Accurate Perception of and high expectations for other people in our lives.

The Pygmalion Effect

The Pygmalion effect comes from the ancient Roman poet Ovid, who told a story about Pygmalion, a sculptor and prince of Cyprus, who created an ivory statue of his ideal woman. The statue, which he called Galatea, was so beautiful that he fell in love with it. He begged the imaginary goddess Aphrodite to breathe life into the statue so that he could make her his own. He believed so strongly that Aphrodite granted Pygmalion his wish. The statue came to life, the couple married and lived happily ever after.

What does this legend have to do with having positive perceptions? Dr. Robert Rosenthal, a Harvard psychologist, and Lenore Jacobson, an elementary school principal, borrowed the term "Pygmalion effect" from the George Bernard Shaw play *Pygmalion*. In the play a professor's high expectations and positive perception of a student transformed her from an average student to a high performer. Some of you may remember that Shaw's play became the basis for the musical *My Fair Lady*. For their study Dr. Rosenthal and Ms. Jacobson sought to examine what happens when we have a positive perception of and high expectations for other people in our lives.

The study participants included all the students in grades one through six of the Oak Hill School in San Francisco. Their teachers were told that the students were taking an intelligence test called the Harvard Test of Inflected Acquisition. This test would determine which students were on the verge of academic excellence. At the conclusion of the test the teachers were informed of all those who scored in the top twenty percent. Little did the teachers realize that the names of the students who they were told scored highest were not based on actual test results, but were instead randomly selected! At the end of the school year all of the children were given an IQ test. The second test was administered to measure any real changes that may have taken place between the students who the teachers thought were smarter, as compared to the students who the teachers were told were average.

The results were fascinating. The students who were randomly "identified" as being in the top twenty-percent early in the school year demonstrated an average increase in their IQ that was 50% higher than the increase measured in the rest of the other students tested!

This finding clearly demonstrates that not only do we need to perceive ourselves as being able to achieve, but also view those around us with this ability as well. Throughout the school year the teacher's perceptions and their higher expectations for those alleged to have more ability did in fact drive those students to higher year-end scores on the intelligence test. When asked, the teachers reported that they perceived these students as brighter, more intellectually curious, happier, and having better personal and social adjustment than the other children. Keep in mind that originally there were absolutely no actual academic differences observed between the two groups!

Everyone Responds To High Expectations

According to another study, an employee's performance in the workplace, like a student's grades at school, is greatly influenced by a manager's expectations of that performance. Researchers at Tel Aviv University demonstrated that employers who expect more from their employees tend to get more! Over a 25-year period they looked not just at schools and businesses, but also at summer camps, banks, and the military. The results were strongly consistent. When the person in charge perceives their subordinates as being highly capable and showers them with high expectations, they succeed! In one study the researchers divided a group of bank branch managers into two groups. The first group was told that their employees were exceptional, while the bank managers in the second group were not told anything about their employees, good or bad. The results showed clearly that the first group of employees outperformed the second group, as was the case with the elementary school children, where prior to the experiment there were no discernible differences in performance between the two groups! The end result was the same. In this case the managers who were told that their employees were exceptional got far more productivity out of those employees. There have been many other experiments that also reveal how high expectations and a positive perception of people bring out the best in those people.

As parents and educators, if we want happier, smarter, and more productive children we must first have a Positive Perception of them as being so. This means treating them as if they are on their way to being successful in school, sports, and every other relationship and facet of their lives. I can't think of a better way to build young lives than with a positive perception of our children. Setting the bar high, and expecting and encouraging them to reach it, will go a long way in helping children become achievers in life. Granted, they won't always succeed, but that's why you're there, to pick them back up, brush them off, and continue feeding them a healthy dose of Positive Expectations!

Similarly, a successful marriage depends as well on a Positive Accurate Perception and high expectations. Take every opportunity to demonstrate the love that you feel toward your spouse. It has been said that we sometimes treat strangers better than we do our loved ones. Is this because we want the stranger to perceive us as kind and considerate? Sometimes when we communicate with someone close to us, we think we can say almost anything. Yet, on the other hand, because we know them so well, we expect them to be gentle in their communication with us. This is a double standard that can cause resentment in the long term. Engage every member of your family in meaningful conversation. Turn off the TV. Talk to one another. Make time for each other. Tell your spouse you love him or her. If you've not yet had a True Vision for creating a more Positive Perception for your family, now is the perfect time to do so. It will pay dividends for years to come in many special ways!

Having a Positive Perception of others is so beneficial that it actually has the power to affect performance in ways that can forever shape lives. But think about this: If having a Positive Perception toward others can help *them* be more productive, can you imagine the great things that a Positive Self-Perception can do for you?

Sandy Scott's Positive Accurate Self-Perception

I had the pleasure of meeting the very high-energy cyclist Sandy Scott, a multiple record holder in his age group. Sandy, now a robust 70-year-old former commercial airline pilot, has demonstrated an incredible Positive Self-Perception. He determined several years ago that he did not want to end up like some of his peers who retired and then died at relatively early ages. "I would look up on the wall and see these memorial plaques to guys who died at 62 or 63. I decided at that moment that was not going to happen to me!" From that point forward his self-perception changed as a True Vision was born. Sandy no longer saw himself as an older guy getting ready for retirement. He launched into a rigorous fitness program, which he maintains to this day, nine years after retirement.

His speed and endurance are awe-inspiring. "Nine months after I took my first pedal stroke I broke the state time trial five kilometer record [for his age group]." Sandy's three best bicycling events have times of 5-K 7:12, 10-K 14:40, 20-K 30:42. **That means that Sandy is able to pedal his bike at the average rate of about 2:35 per mile for over 12 continuous miles, at the age of 70!** Think about that for just a few seconds. At an age when many people are considering which retirement home to live out the remainder of their years, Sandy Scott is competing with and beating cycle racers, not only in his age group but those who are less than half his age!

"I've ridden with some really top guys from every age group and I'm the one usually leading the way. What's fun is I've been in this sport a very short time and I've already knocked off a couple of Olympians, and a string of national champions. I was riding with the 'A' group recently and I'm usually leading the sprint at the end. I have these kids coming up to me and asking me what Olympics I was in [he wasn't]. One college rider that I beat at the end said to me 'I can't believe that I can't beat a 70 year old.' I told him jokingly, maybe you should give up the sport." That's one college kid who may think twice the next time he mounts his bike and looks across the line only to see someone who might look like a grandfather.

For all of you workout aficionados, in addition to Sandy's prolific bicycling he has also performed 20 repetition squats with a barbell loaded to 225 pounds! For those of you who have a difficult time appreciating this feat by a 5'11", 150 pound, 70-year-old man, all you have to do is to try performing something called free squats (squats with no weight on your back). Squat down until your upper legs break parallel with the knees, and then back up keeping your back straight. When you get to 20 you will better understand Sandy Scott's conditioning. Absolutely incredible! (A cautionary note: I'm sure Sandy began his Herculean fitness regime gradually. Make sure you are examined by your doctor prior to performing this or any sort of strenuous exercise.)

I asked Sandy why he feels that he is able to perform at such a high level at the age of 70. His response was not surprising: "A big percentage of physical performance is mental strength, not physical strength. Visualization techniques are something that I've used all my life. As an example, when I was an airline pilot we had to take a very comprehensive oral, physical and flying exam. I would sit there and visualize the entire test, every detail. I knew exactly what I wanted to do. I did the same thing when it came to [bicycle] racing. I know exactly what I am going to do, what speed I am going to average, and even how it will feel before I enter the race. I go over the course ahead of time and then visualize every part of it before the race begins. I always visualize myself winning, and it becomes a self-fulfilling prophecy. Some racers see me and say 'Well I guess I'm racing for second place today.' I think, you're darn right you are, because you just defeated yourself with that self-fulfilling prophecy. I have a Vision to be the best in the United States and I'm going to fulfill that Vision!" I think he will do just that!

Sandy recognizes that performance is tied to good nutrition and is a strong believer in vitamin supplements. He usually takes his nutrients in the morning. They include a multi-vitamin, vitamin C, fish oil, vitamin D, and some other nutrients. He also eats dark unsweetened chocolate as a snack later in the day. Sandy consumes fish twice a week and holds red meat consumption to a minimum. He makes sure he gets eight hours of sleep a night. "I feel the difference when I don't get those eight hours. Sleep is so important. The pituitary gland produces the body's natural hormones when you are in a deep sleep." I think Sandy has formed impressive Winning Habits on his way to so many victories. I also admire how he refuses to use the Shield of Excuse when it comes to age: "One of the problems with people is that they limit themselves because of age. Some people might say, jeez I'm 70 years old. I better watch it and not exert myself." Sandy then explained that this is a self-fulfilling prophecy that proves itself to be true by the believer's will to make it happen.

Sandy's Positive Self-Perception is that of a much younger man, but how much younger I wondered? So before ending our conversation I had to ask Sandy one more question. "How old would you be if you didn't know how old you were?" Since I have never known anyone like

Sandy I was curious about how old he felt most of the time. Obviously, his self-perception is that of a much younger person, but I wanted specifics. "I am not 70, I would never consider myself 70," he replied. "Then how old are you Sandy?" I asked again. There was dead silence. I ask again, a bit differently. "Aside from cycling. Let's say you're going to the grocery store, you're out shopping, doing day to day activities. In general, during the average course of the day, away from your sport, how old do you feel?" "Overall I'm in better shape now than I was when I was younger. I have so much energy I don't know what to do with myself. My blood cholesterol is lower than it was 30 years ago, I'm more vascular, I have a body fat percentage of 3.9%, my HDL [the good cholesterol] is off the charts high." This still did not answer my question. I ask for a final time, "Sandy, how old would you be if you didn't know how old you were?" After another brief silence he finally responded, "After thinking about it, I would say 42." 42? I wondered to myself how many 42-year old men could keep up with Sandy Scott either on, or off, a bike? This is one man who really is living his True Vision! If you want to read more about Sandy Scott you can buy his book: *From Broken Neck To Broken Records: A Masters Cyclist's Guide to Winning.*

Sandy Scott perceives himself as a 42-year-old. How old do you perceive yourself to be? If you had to be able to back it up, just as Sandy did, with your lifestyle habits and vital signs, where would you be then? If you are thinking that one reason why Sandy Scott is in such incredible condition is because he has good genetics, I would agree with you. It takes good genes to do what he is doing. But keep in mind he would not have even been aware of his genetic potential had he not first had a True Vision for fitness along with a Positive Self-Perception.

I wonder how many people have such great genetics yet never realize it because they never developed such a Positive Self-Perception?

Now just because Sandy is able to pedal his way to multiple state racing titles does not mean that you can, or should. But it also doesn't mean that you cannot. Nor does it mean that you are unable to simply improve, regardless of how far you go. In other words, Sandy is the best that he can be: are you? Telling yourself that he is a certain way because of genetics does not help you! It only gives you a Shield of Excuse to not try!

If you are in reasonable condition and have been cleared by your doctor for exercise, what stops you from maximizing your own potential, whatever that might be? If all you can do currently is walk once around the block then that is a great beginning. You can raise your own Self-Perception by gradually adding a little distance to that walk. If you are thinking that it will take you too long to get into really good condition, I can only remind you that the time is going to pass anyway, and what will you have to show for it? You do not want to be sitting here next year thinking that you could have made a positive transformation in your life and did not do it, do you?

You may never be at Sandy's fitness level, few are at any age. The good news is that you do not have to be! You only have to be as good as you can be. You purchased this book because you have your sights set on something more for your life. Maybe you have a totally different True Vision. Let Sandy's great example of a Positive Self-Perception and maximum fitness serve to inspire you to cultivate a True Vision for a Positive Self-Perception of your own. If it also leads to your maximum fitness, then all the better. If it leads you to losing 30 pounds and fitting into clothes you haven't worn in years, then that is great too, isn't it? Keep in mind that this is your True Vision. Cultivating a Positive Self-Perception will certainly help turn that Vision into a reality!

View Your Self-Perception Through a Clear Lens

If we perceive ourselves as successful at what we do, we have a far better chance of succeeding at it. It could be because there is a strong connection between having a Positive Perception of success and the amount of effort that we put forward in attempting to achieve our True Vision. In other words, if you truly believe that all of the work you put toward your True Vision will ultimately pay off, you will put more work into your True Vision, which will then assure that it does pay off! Do you have a Positive Perception of your own reality like Sandy Scott does? Or, do you have a distorted unhealthy perception, which has been harming your chance of achieving your True Vision?

Some people imagine a history of perceived failure, which can also distort their perception of their current reality. Does this describe you, or someone you know? How many times have you half-heartedly tried to do something, and when you failed chalked it up to your lack of ability and talent? Were you being fair and accurate in judging yourself, or were you being overly harsh, changing your perception of yourself from accurate to inaccurate? After all, how many people actually succeed at something with a half-hearted effort? Even your best effort can sometimes fail to give you what you're looking for the first time around.

When you perceive the world as too difficult and yourself as inadequate, nothing good can come from such an assessment. When you view your life from a distorted lens, you bend your perception of reality in a direction that puts you at an extreme disadvantage. Why would you work against yourself? Does that make sense? This is the perfect time to turn around false misconceptions that you may have lived with for a period of time. Begin to view the world with a Positive Accurate Perception, as that view is not only more realistic, but will also help you to succeed. It's time to perceive yourself as a competent and unique individual who has the capacity to achieve his True Vision!

The next time you feel that you failed at something, I want you to take another look at it. Play detective, think back to how your temporary set-back was given birth. Try to remember the approach that you took, and how you felt as it unraveled. Did you really give it your best sustained effort? Was it a smart, well-thought-out plan, or something that you rushed into? Did you use Effective Communication and ask those that might have helpful insight and experience in this particular area for advice? Or, did you already think that you knew all there was to know? Did you use the Urgency Factor from the beginning? Or did you let time pass before you took concerted action? Did you act with Positive Self-Discipline, or give in to a short-term gain for a long-term loss? Did you create Winning Habits, which would have caused you to build on your success? Did you use Total Focus on this plan at its inception, which would have caused your Vision to immediately increase in importance and stature? Did you create Positive Accurate Perceptions for yourself and all of those people whom you touch each day? Most importantly, did you begin with a red-hot True Vision constantly playing in the theater of your mind?

Be fair in your analysis. If the answer to any of these questions is "no" then it might be time to look closer at your frame of mind. It is difficult indeed to view yourself with a Positive Self-Perception when you are in a sad, mad, or scared state of mind much of the time. Let's next look at some techniques to get you in the Glad Frame of Mind, which will increase your chances of not only achieving your True Vision, but also of being happy while you're on the way there!

chapter ten

VISION STEP:
GLAD, SAD, MAD OR SCARED?

The emotions aren't always immediately subject to reason,
but they are always immediately subject to action.
  —William James

The Four Basic Emotional States

There are only four basic emotional states: Glad, Sad, Mad, and Scared. Every emotion that we have is either one of those four, or some combination of them. When we're in what I call the Glad Frame of Mind we are more open to new possibilities. We tend toward the explorative, creative, and positive. Most importantly, we feel more able to control a good part of our destiny when we are Glad as opposed to being sad, mad, or scared. It's usually best to be in the Glad Frame of Mind (we will discuss how to get there later in the chapter), and many positive things can be generated in this state. Even so, very dramatic and positive change also comes from feeling the stress of one or more of the other three states, sad, mad or scared.

For example, if you are in debt, and it's bothering you, you might be feeling one or more of these emotions. But they can also be the very impetus for change! If you are satisfied with your life, and live it daily in a Glad state, there is no real desire for change, is there? Positive, dramatic change in your life usually comes from a deep place of distress. None of us ever looks forward to feeling that stress in the form of being sad, mad or scared, as these states can be unpleasant. Nonetheless, it is when we find ourselves mired in these emotional states that we become motivated to make changes that can be long lasting. Eventually (sooner than you think) the changes we make get us to the Glad Frame of Mind!

Carl Jung, the eminent Swiss psychoanalyst, said, "There can be no transforming of darkness into light, and of apathy into movement without emotion." Where does that deep well of emotion come from which ultimately triggers the desire for change? Generally it comes from a dark place. Put another way, if you are perfectly satisfied with your life one hundred percent of the time (Glad Frame) why would you attempt to change anything? Yet, if you are aware that part of your life is not satisfying to you, then there now exists a reason to change.

Let's take for example a person who is unhappy with her job. She trudges in to work every day, just putting in her time. She is half-trying most of the time because she is basically unhappy with what she is doing. From her emotional mind-set she can either lash out at her family or friends (displaced aggression), or she can internalize these emotions, which could end up manifesting themselves through migraine headaches, digestive issues, back and neck pain, and so on. In fact, many medical authorities believe that up to 90% of all disease comes from or is exacerbated by stress!

The obvious and most positive way to deal with her anger (mad state) is to find another job or to think about a career change. Once she realizes this, she must go through the process of repeatedly visualizing herself in another position, one that is a better fit for her, so that she can avoid making a poor decision and end up back where she had started. At this point she has taken the first step in creating her True Vision, which can lead her to a career opportunity that will put her in the Glad Frame of Mind. In other words, for her the process will begin first through being mad enough at her situation to make a change.

There is nothing wrong with experiencing the emotions mad, sad, or scared regarding a part of your life that is not satisfying to you. That is because these emotions can act as a catalyst that ultimately propels you toward your True Vision and long-term happiness (being Glad). Do you remember Kendra and Cindy, the women earlier in the book who were respectively trying to lose weight and stop smoking? Both experienced fear at some point during the process that helped them move away from the thing that scared them, and toward their True Vision. In fact, I tried to introduce negative visual images to help each of them associate a negative outcome with the very thing that each wanted to be free of. When we look deeply and introspectively at our emotions, we become more honest about our lives and the behaviors that are preventing us from achieving our True Vision. These emotions, when seen for what they actually represent, will ultimately help us achieve the changes we want.

The Dentons Go From Mad To Glad

Wayne and Rebecca Denton were not thinking about which state of mind they were in when they were spending money they didn't have. However, when they realized they were $88,000 in debt they immediately became very scared! Eventually, they felt both sad (when it came time to try to pay the bills) and mad enough to make a change as they realized where they actually needed to be at that point in their financial lives. "These were normal expenses. We didn't take nice vacations, we didn't drive fancy cars. We were paying off two cars, a student loan and some credit card debt. When you're not making enough money to pay your bills and you end up behind paying late fees, it just snowballs," said Rebecca.

She decided one day that the snowball had rolled far enough down the hill. She was mad, and that ignited the Urgency Factor! "We got mad at our debt, we took a look at what we were spending, and decided to make a change." Rebecca told me that one of the first actions that she took was to cut up her credit cards. "My husband, bless his heart, came home from work, and all of our credit cards were cut up. So he wasn't exactly a willing participant in the beginning." Rebecca went on to say, "I don't recommend doing that. At first he wasn't really happy. In fact the debt itself put a huge strain on our marriage." Her second course of action was to sell everything that was not nailed down in order to raise $1,000 for an emergency fund. "We went through everything in our house, our attic, every drawer, every nook and cranny. We had so much stuff we didn't need that we set up a gigantic yard sale. I even sold my husband's underwear! He wasn't still in them so I figured there'd be no problem." Rebecca went on to say that her husband Wayne was complaining, not about losing his underwear, but that "no one was going to buy this stuff. We ended up making over $1,000 that day!" she recalled.

"Maybe it was the way we marketed it, 'everything but Granny's panties.' Well, at least Granny got to keep her underwear. Poor Wayne, I wish I could say the same for him.

Obviously, the Dentons understood that they needed more than just a yard sale to pay down the mountain of debt they had accumulated. "I then started working a whole bunch of overtime shifts. I figured out how many overtime shifts I had to work in order to help get us out debt; it was about 114. I had a calendar on the refrigerator, and just like a child in school marking off the days until summer vacation, I would track my progress." Rebecca, who is a nurse, worked sixteen hours of overtime a week. Her husband Wayne, working a full-time job that with travel time added up to a sixty-hour week, also did most of the housework. It was very much a joint effort. "I have to be in control of my money, or my money will control me," she reflected. When asked what advice Rebecca could give to those in the same position as they were, she said: "We're real people with average paying jobs. It takes hard work, and you have to pay attention to it. Instead of being bitter, overwhelmed, and frustrated by the debt, do something about it! Get mad about it. Work your day job and deliver pizzas at night if you have to. There are ways that you can find to get out of debt."

Bankruptcy, interestingly enough, was not an option for the Denton's. "We spent the money and wanted to pay it back." Rebecca and Wayne Denton are average people who are an inspiration to those Americans who are faced with a similar crushing debt load. They took the negative emotions of mad, sad, and scared, and turned their lives around by mastering the basics. They are both to be admired for their efforts, but their message to you is that if they can do it, so can you! If you find yourself experiencing the emotions of mad, sad or scared over a debt problem here is the path to freedom:

15 Steps To A Debt Free Life

1. Practice Effective Communication techniques with your spouse or debt partner regarding all financial matters. Withholding information from one another will not help. But make sure that you are not squabbling about debt on a daily basis. Set time aside each week in one specific neutral area of the house to discuss finances, not the bedroom or the kitchen. If you have no spouse or partner then it is time to stop lying to yourself!

2. There are few people who have serious debt problems who do not have credit cards. Not everyone should have a credit card. If you have a debt problem right now there is a good chance that you should not have that card, so get rid of it!

3. Raise as much money as you can to pay down your debt. In the Dentons' case they had a large yard sale. Do you have a basement or garage full of money?

4. Earn more money. This can be done as the Dentons did by working overtime and using the proceeds to pay down debt. It can also be done by getting a part-time job or even starting a part-time, or full-time business using the skills that you already possess to earn more money to help pay down your debt. However, keep in mind that you must fix your overspending habit first. You will never be able to earn your way out of a bad spending habit!

5. Begin to pay off all debts, either smallest to largest (when you see one debt disappear you will have immediate gratification), or highest interest rate first, followed by the next, and so on. Pay extra down on those remaining when you can.

6. Create a sound budget process that you stay with.

7. Stop taking a Short-Term gain (which is the immediate gratification of spending). This only gives you a Long-Term loss (racking up debt) which could eventually destroy you.

8. Understand that more material possessions will not make you happier in the long-term. Material possessions will not make you nearly as happy as the eventual high debt will make you sad. Reread the section in the book on lottery winners, and learn from their mistakes.

9. Establish a True Vision regarding your financial life. If you plan ahead for possible financial emergencies you will be ready if they come. That means saving just a bit from every paycheck. Start with just 10% and see if you can eventually go beyond that figure.

10. Never Give Up! Always keep trying to make your life better. It is true that nothing in life is guaranteed. But I can guarantee one thing: if you give up you will never win. When people give up they sometimes tend to spiral down into a further negative state.

11. Change happens gradually. You most likely didn't get into a serious debt problem overnight. You will not get out of it overnight either. Be patient.

12. Focus on the problem, don't ignore it. Whatever you apply Total Focus to usually improves, and whatever you ignore usually gets worse.

13. Employ the Urgency Factor. Deal with the problem right now before it gets worse. If you think you have a debt problem now, how is ignoring it for even one more day going to help?

14. Have a realistic perception of debt, for being in debt can become a very powerful force that can tear you apart emotionally, end your marriage, and ruin your life!

15. Each time that you pay off a debt or gain extra household income have a mini-celebration. Get a blueberry muffin, put a candle on top and make sure your anthem is playing in the background. Each celebration of such a milestone will encourage you to stay the course.

Before we move on I want to make a comparison between getting out of debt and losing weight. The person who is attempting to lose weight needs to burn more calories than they consume. In order to accomplish this there are two important variables: the consumption of calories and the movement which burns them.

The person trying to get out of debt must spend less than they earn. The two important variables here are: working more hours (or getting a higher rate of pay) to increase income, and reducing consumption of things not essential.

Interestingly enough they both frequently have to do with extravagance. The first is a choice to consume additional calories, the second to purchase additional goods and services. In both cases the additional consumption is not a necessity, but rather a choice in which Positive Self-Discipline has not been properly applied. By applying Positive Self-Discipline and adjusting just two variables you have created a Winning Habit and are on your way to achieving your True Vision!

What are you facing today? How can you use the pain of being in the mad, sad or scared frame of mind to create a True Vision for change in your life?

Getting In The Glad Frame Of Mind

Being mad, sad, or scared can incite change and can therefore work to your advantage. However, it is far more pleasant and productive to be in the Glad Frame of Mind (GFOM) for the long-term!

In fact, being able to put yourself in the GFOM is one of the most important Vision Steps that you can accomplish! For without being in the GFOM you will most likely find it more difficult to utilize all of the other Vision Step skills. In addition, not being in the GFOM in general is a most unpleasant and, long-term, unproductive way to live your life.

For example, trying to function efficiently in the mad frame of mind will not help you live out your True Vision. Being sad, mad, or scared could be the spark which ignites your True Vision. However, just like the spark that ignites your car's engine, after it serves its purpose it ceases to exist. Remaining in one of those negative states in the long-term is not at all emotionally healthy or productive. This is especially so once you are on your way to accomplishing your True Vision. Why would anyone actually want to be in the sad, mad, or scared state of mind anyway? Yet, if you take a close look at the population there are many who seem to bounce around between the sad, mad, and scared states far more than they should. When a person is in one of these more negative states, he or she is most likely feeling one (or more) of the following emotions:

Annoyed—Angry—Afraid—Ashamed—Awkward—Confused—Defeated—Disappointed—Distrustful—Embarrassed—Grief—Guilt—Hopeless—Irritated—Impatient—Insecure—Jealous—Nervous—Regret—Uncertain—Worried.

I think that it is obvious that being in one or more of these states for a prolonged period of time can cause emotional (and possibly physical) pain. Once again, using one of these states as an agent for change is a good thing. Dwelling in one of these states daily is a negative, self-defeating way to live your life. And it becomes extremely difficult, if not impossible, to accomplish your True Vision when you are spending much of your time between the sad, mad and scared frames of mind.

Various emotions felt when we are in the GFOM:

Affectionate—Accepted—Able—Content—Confident—Competent—
Eager—Fulfilled—Generous—Hopeful—Honored—Humorous—
Joyous—Love—Pride—Peaceful—Relieved—Respected—Relaxed—
Secure—Strong—Satisfied.

I'm sure you'll agree from this list that being in the GFOM is where you want to be. Once you are on your way toward achieving your True Vision for success, being in the GFOM is what will help you succeed long-term. For example, when we feel able, confident, eager and hopeful we're more apt to fight on and never give up. We also feel very good about ourselves and enjoy life a whole lot more!

Since we know that it is better long-term to be in the GFOM, let's take a look at various strategies for getting you in the GFOM, and staying there!

Strategies For Getting In The Glad Frame Of Mind: People Both Positive And Negative

Let's begin with people. If you have the wrong people in your life, those that cause you unnecessary stress and emotional pain for example, it becomes difficult to get in and remain in the GFOM. We all have people in our lives who make us feel good, and then there are those who almost immediately put us in the sad, mad, or scared frame. I'm sure you have been around people like this; I know I have. It doesn't matter why the person makes you feel stressed. It could be that they come off as a "know it all," and think they have every answer that you can imagine to help you with that one big problem you have. Yet, their own personal and professional life is in a shambles. Then there is the type that wants to talk all about themselves, their spouse, their children, their job, and their life. You exist only as an audience to stroke their ego. Still others just want to talk about everyone else, and they never seem to have anything good to say about anyone or anything. Then there is the person who is constantly borrowing something from you. It could be anything from money, to tools, or even clothes, with never a thought to give it back. You're his or her best friend only when he or she needs something. Some people leave you feeling like you'd rather not have bumped into them, much less actually planned to spend time with them. These types of people can cause you anxiety (scared state), irritate you (mad state), or simply leave you in the sad state of mind. Your reasonable expectations will never be met by these people—and it is time to rethink these relationships.

Are you really better off with these people in your life? These types are usually not the kinds of people who will help you, or are even open to real help from you. They are not looking to advance your life or even theirs in a positive way. They may not think that advancement in any particular area is even possible without stepping on others. They deplete your energy, your emotions, and your reserves. Ask yourself, what is the point of these relationships? If they don't put you in the GFOM, or have some other positive reason for existence, what is the point? You might just be better off without them in your life.

As for the special case of relatives, you may have a close relative who regularly depends on your support in some way—a child or a disabled or elderly parent. There are instances where you are needed to bring joy to others by helping to put them in the GFOM, and we should give them our best. However, there are relatives who simply take from you in the form of energy, time, and money, and never seem to either appreciate it, get any better, or return the favor. If this puts you in the GFOM, then certainly continue on. However, more than likely they stir negative emotions and it could be time to at least cut back on the contact that you have with these people, or have a heart to heart talk in hopes of salvaging the relationship by setting up new boundaries. You might find that after doing this you spend more time in the GFOM.

What is the point of friendship or even friendly relationships? Friends should have things in common, be looking out for the betterment of one another, and build each other up. It should be a two-way street. A mutual admiration should be evident. If those things are missing, what is the point of the relationship? When you say "yes" to spending time with negative types of people, you are automatically saying "no" to others who will help put you in the GFOM and perhaps further your True Vision. There are only so many hours in a day. With whom shall you spend them?

Positive Relationships

We know when we are involved in a positive relationship because we almost always feel good about it, not only when we are with that person, but also when we walk away. We feel refreshed, rejuvenated, entertained, sometimes even enlightened, but we always feel something positive. I'm sure you know exactly what I mean. One such person in my life is retired from a church I used to attend. His name is Pastor Richard Parelli. We used to get together once or twice a week. I would put him through a rigorous workout, sometimes to prepare him for ski season, other times we would train just for fun. It was because of his great wisdom, knowledge, and sense of humor that I always felt reinvigorated after our training sessions. He was, and remains, a builder of people. Unlike others in his field, he came from a business background so we enjoyed sharing various business experiences. If I presented an idea to him he would contemplate it and respond with a very thoughtful insight. I always marveled at the depth and breadth of his wisdom. He relocated away from my area, and I felt the sudden impact on my life, a void. While I still consider him a friend, I wish I had put more of an effort into staying in contact. Have you ever made such a mistake?

If you are fortunate enough to have such people in your life, try to spend more time with them. This may seem obvious, but sometimes it requires a direct effort on your part or the friendship slips away, and you are the worse for it. Search out those rare individuals who are able through wisdom, humor, and knowledge, or simply by shared interests, to put you in the GFOM. One more benefit is that when you are spending time with those who create this positive state in you, you are not spending time with those who place you in one of the more negative states.

If you purposely spend time with people whose warmth, intelligence and humor make you feel good, you will automatically spend more time in the GFOM. I am not advising that you should completely avoid people who take you out of the GFOM, but reducing the amount of time that you are with them can be done easily. I know this may seem obvious, but the question is, do you practice it? If you don't focus on this you will not get the benefit. For the next 30 days purposely try to fill your spare time with people who put you in the GFOM, and you will see exactly what I am talking about!

Activities That Put You In The GFOM

We have only twenty-four hours in a day, and they have to be filled with something. Why can't that "something" be activities that put you in the GFOM? What are the best ways to accomplish that? Let's take a look at what science and experience have to say about the best possible activities to put you in the GFOM.

Let's begin with something that is highly underrated, but if not looked at as important, can literally ruin your life! I am talking about sleep.

Importance Of Sleep

How sleep rejuvenates the body is still a mystery; however, we do know that if we don't get enough sleep, for even one night, it becomes more difficult to function properly the next day. It has been proven that your GFOM is directly related to how well you sleep. When we don't sleep well, or sleep long enough, our serotonin level, which helps control our emotional balance, drops.

There have been reliable surveys which have discovered that people who have six or less hours of sleep per night do not achieve as high a mood rating as those who have had seven to nine hours of sleep. It seems that there are some very important neurotransmitters in the brain which are directly affected by sleep. When these important neurotransmitters are adversely affected by lack of sleep your mood can also be negatively impacted.

Sleep is so important that one indicator of depression is having a sleep disorder of some type. While a sleep disorder may indicate depression, the reverse of this might also be true. That is, sleep disorders such as insomnia may actually cause mood disorders and depression! In short, not getting enough of the proper kind of sleep could put you in the **sad** frame of mind, and keep you there.

The research is fairly consistent. When we cheat ourselves out of our much needed eight hours of sleep a night, we leave ourselves open not only to being in the **sad** frame of mind, but also to many other negative things. Lack of sleep affects memory and the ability to concentrate, and these shortages can place you in the **mad** frame of mind as you fight to remember things that seem to be just on the tip of your tongue. Have you ever had that experience? There have been many studies which point out the risks of driving while sleep deprived. In fact, driving while sleep deprived increases your chance of being in an accident. Recent studies have demonstrated that your motor coordination is so reduced while driving in a sleep-deprived state that it is similar to driving while under the influence of alcohol! Lack of sleep also harms the immune system. Many studies have shown that our immune system is negatively impacted when we are sleep-deprived, which leaves us more susceptible to colds, flu and even worse!

It is easy to see that having a lack of concentration, losing motor coordination, and possibly developing a sickness will certainly not put you in the GFOM. Happily, these are things that are well within your ability to control.

11 Ideas For A Better Night's Sleep

1. Certain things that we eat or drink before bed can interfere with sleep. For example, alcohol, while it may help you get to sleep, contrary to popular belief negatively affects sleep patterns as it may cause you to wake suddenly after falling asleep.

2. No surprise with the following: Caffeine and nicotine, which stimulate the nervous system, should be off limits up to four hours before bed.

3. Exercising in the four hours or less before bed can keep you awake. However, exercising early in the day can actually help you get to sleep and you will have a more restful sleep.

4. Napping is not usually a good idea unless it is a short nap, less than thirty-minutes before 4:00 p.m. If you sleep any longer or later in the day, you may not feel tired at your normal bedtime and you will stay up later. This will make you more tired the next day, which in turn encourages you to take a longer nap, further throwing off your sleep cycle. Napping does this by upsetting your natural circadian rhythm (your body's regular cycles that govern hunger, alertness, various hormones, and body temperature). I have a friend who had this problem and I advised her to avoid taking a nap the following day when she had slept only four hours the night before. She took my advice, and after a couple of nights with very little sleep she turned her sleeping pattern around. Following a hectic schedule can cause occasional sleep disturbances to happen to all of us periodically.

5. Sleep in a dark room. Light too can affect your circadian rhythm. While you may sleep for eight hours you will wake not feeling rested.

6. Sometimes we are so involved in our day that it's difficult to turn our mental attention away from its concerns or the next day's schedule, and relax. I have a good technique that has worked well for me for many years. I keep a pad and pen next to my bed and jot down everything I want to do the next day, and perhaps things that I should have done on that day. Once it is written it is mentally released from my mind and I am able to relax. If I've had a particularly hectic day I will sometimes awake at night with an idea that happens to come to mind and, without turning on the light, I will jot it down on my bedside pad. When I first started doing this I had no idea what I had written. The following day it looked like a three-year-old had scribbled on a piece of paper. It was actually good for a chuckle or two. After a few weeks of practice, when I looked at my notes the next day I could actually read an idea that I had written down in the dark, in the middle of the night. Once again, everything is difficult before it gets easy!

7. As I stated in the chapter on Positive Perception, I believe the reporting of the news is structured to be sensational. This is done in order to catch your attention and keep you watching. Unfortunately, most of this sensationalism is very negative. Certainly if this bothers you, stay away from hard news before you go to bed. Better to watch an old movie, listen to relaxing music, or read a calming book. Look for activities that can put you in the GFOM. You will not only improve the quality of your sleep, you will also awake with a more positive attitude.

8. If you take medication for whatever reason, check the side effects. Some medications can cause insomnia. If this is a problem for you, consult your doctor to see if it is okay to take that particular medication earlier in the day. This might be all you have to do to get the proper amount and quality of sleep.

9. Having a light snack an hour or two before bedtime is sometimes a good idea, something with complex carbohydrates which can soothe you. One good source of complex carbohydrates can be found in whole grains. A good snack before bed might be a high fiber grain cereal. Mom's old remedy of warm milk and cookies can be modified. How about warm milk and a small raisin oat bran or blueberry muffin made with natural ingredients? This

will not only relax you, but can also prevent you from awaking during the night with hunger pangs. Just remember to keep it light.

10. Sometimes we cannot get to sleep because our thoughts are far too structured. You are thinking about work, relationships and other things of importance in your life, and even though you wrote them down earlier you just cannot let go. One technique that may work is to switch off the logical mind and try to think of nonsensical thoughts. That might be one reason counting sheep jumping over a fence actually works. You can try that, or you can make up something of your own, like flying sheep, or flying cows, or cows flying airplanes. Just make sure that whatever you are thinking makes no sense at all. Flying sheep, cats and dogs playing pool, bubble gum clouds floating past, trees that grow up through the clouds into space—this may seem bizarre, but it works! This technique will disengage the logical part of your brain while engaging your more creative silly side. As soon as your thoughts begin to make no sense, you will fall asleep, as you are no longer exercising that intense concern over whatever might be keeping you up. Like any technique, the more you practice the better you get at it, and the faster you will fall asleep!

11. Above all do not try to force yourself to go to sleep; it will have the reverse effect, as you've probably already discovered. Just like trying to grab a handful of water, it cannot be done. But you can use your hand to gently scoop a handful of water. Take the same approach when you seem to be faced with a mild case of insomnia, which happens to almost everyone on occasion. When this happens to me I will try to see how late I can stay up. This sounds counter-intuitive, I know. It's a mind game that works to reverse the thought that I have to get to sleep. I will lie in bed and take deep breaths (see the section on meditation and deep breathing) while trying to stay awake. About 90% of the time I will fall asleep almost immediately. If you feel this is not working and become frustrated, get up and read, or work on something productive. One time I didn't get to sleep until 5:00 a.m. and had to get up two hours later. I didn't take a nap that day, and slept for a solid nine hours that night! The point is to relax. If you don't get enough sleep for one or two nights, you will the

following night. Your body has a way of getting what it needs eventually. The only reason it might not is if you start worrying about getting enough sleep. It is important to make sleep a priority, but it is a mistake to worry about it!

Sleep is highly underrated, yet it is something that not only places you in the GFOM, but also helps to keep you healthy physically. **In fact, I believe that the quality of your life is to a large extent determined by the quality of your sleep.** Yes, it is that important! You have to make a commitment to really try to make sleep a priority and to increase the quality and length of your sleep each night. You will find that you are in the GFOM more often, and we know that is a state of mind where your enjoyment of life can greatly improve!

Movement Is Fun

Exercise is a scary word for some people. Instead think of it simply as movement. Do you move around enough during the day? A formal exercise regime is not necessary in order to benefit from movement. Some people may work physically demanding jobs, or are on the go virtually the entire day. You may not like exercise, but if you like to move around that is all that exercise really is and you will experience the benefit! There is almost nothing better to put you in the GFOM than movement. You don't need to join a gym, or sign up for aerobics at your local YMCA, although both would be beneficial. You simply need to move around for thirty minutes five times per week (more if you have the inclination). It doesn't matter if you do this at your job, at home, at a gym, in your backyard or neighborhood, or anywhere else. From this point forward try to think differently about exercise. It is simply movement, and everyone needs to move!

People have been taught that they need to form an exercise "routine" and stay on it. That is absolutely unnecessary and might even produce the exact opposite result of what you set out to do. In fact, that sort of teaching has discouraged more people from exercise than almost anything else I can think of. It's almost like going on a diet. If you go on a diet, that means that eventually you go off it. That is one reason that diets rarely work in the long-term. The long-term answer to weight loss is rarely found by going on a diet. Similarly, creating an exercise routine is one of the worst ways to stay in shape long-term because you will invariably go off the routine as you become bored. When boredom sets in it's only a matter of time before the final exercise you perform is to walk away from your "routine." In addition, unless you keep your program fluid and varied your body adjusts to the same movements. One more problem of a regular routine is that you become susceptible to repetitive stress injury by performing the same boring exercises repeatedly. Any doubt that aggressive exercise movements repeated continuously over a long period of time can cause injury should not be questioned. Overuse is all that is needed for you to become injured, and many workout routines are very suspect in that area.

Instead of a routine, simply wake up one day and choose to move around more. Does that sound too easy? If you want to stick to traditional workout venues, go to the gym but do something totally different each day, and have fun. If the person at the gym tells you that you must be on a routine, tell him or her that your routine is having no routine. Make sure you smile when you say that, and keep walking as they are talking to you, since movement is part of your "routine." I rarely have a set routine in my own training, unless I am aiming for some sort of personal best or training for a record of some kind. If I am not making a specific record attempt then my training is based completely on varied movement, having fun, and what I feel like doing on any particular day. Certainly many of my training sessions are very physically taxing. You can make these movement sessions as difficult or as easy as you would like, as long as you enjoy them.

Shouldn't exercise be fun? When you were a child you used to get all of the exercise that you needed and you never realized that you were exercising, did you? I want you to create a similar environment for yourself as an adult. For example, I have a large slide that I use on occasion as part of my creative exercise. I sprint up the stairway of the slide as fast as I can, slide down, and then slow jog to the stairs and do it again. I may do this ten times or so and then climb a rope several times or do chin-ups on a nearby tree. After about thirty minutes I am through and in the GFOM! It's fun because I wanted to be outside in the fresh air and I trained the way I wanted to that day and it was beneficial. The next time, I will probably do something entirely different depending on how I feel. I may do something that specifically involves strength. You don't need expensive equipment or to belong to a gym. All you need to do is move!

You can work on moving around more by yourself, or get together with people that you enjoy being with and just play games. It could be anything from playing tennis one day to basketball the next. It doesn't matter how well you play either. All that matters is that you are moving around. In the beginning it's just the movement that you are after. If you end up getting really good at a particular sport, fine, if that's what you want. But more importantly, during the process of playing you are going to be moving around, breaking a sweat, getting in shape, and having fun. Again constant change is what you're after, especially when it stops being fun. After watching so many fail at exercise routines I realized that variety and control over that variety are what will keep you interested, and will also prevent you from burning out. Make sure that you don't get overly concerned about when you are going to have your sessions. Avoid getting into a routine unless of course you love the routine, and it encourages you to come back and do more. The most important point is to keep moving. For example, if you are playing frisbee, throw a few to your partner where he has to run to catch it, and encourage him to do the same for you. Better yet, play a game called walking frisbee. You and your partner must keep walking while you are throwing the Frisbee back and forth. It's fun, and you will break a sweat faster than you can imagine.

Before beginning any exercise program, especially if you have been inactive for a long period of time, you should consult with your physician. He may want to monitor your progress. Speaking with your doctor first is very important!

The following is a short list of ideas for moving around which will help you get the sort of exercise that will put you in the GFOM. In addition to tennis, basketball, and frisbee, try swimming, tag, walking the dog, walking while carrying a weighted object. Anything will do (expensive equipment not needed, and don't let the neighbors giving you funny looks bother you). See how many push-ups you can do one day, and then try to top that a few days later. Of course, you can do this with any movement. See how far you can park your car from where you want to go and still get there on time. Make a vegetable garden in your backyard. Rake the leaves. Mow the lawn with a non-power push mower. If you are watching TV, every time a commercial comes on do some sit-ups, push-ups, leg raises, side bends, free squats (squats without a barbell), or even shadow box until your show comes back on. If you live in a two-story house or apartment keep a pad and pencil by the stairs and write down how many times you climb the stairs that day. When you go to the supermarket keep your cart in one place and go find each item that you need without your cart. When both hands are full return to your cart and then go off again in search of the next item(s). Fill your cart that way. If you have a desk job, instead of taking a coffee break take a brief movement break. Take a walk or perform any combination of movements for ten minutes.

According to the Centers for Disease Control (CDC) if you are a healthy adult between the ages of 18 and 64 you need to exercise for thirty minutes five days a week. If you fill this minimum requirement you will be ahead of over 80% of the population in terms of fitness. But keep trying to push yourself to do more, and if you are having fun this should be easy to do. On the other hand, if you experience any pain or discomfort, stop immediately and see your doctor. The list of ways to move is endless. It is only limited by your ability to be creative.

I would love to give you a detailed explanation of fitness, and of how an average person can do incredible things with more serious dedication, the proper training, and, of course, nutrition. A serious discussion of fitness would be quite involved, and unfortunately it is beyond the scope of this book. For now I want you to focus on movement, as that is the key which can turn the lock to your own positive emotional and physical transformation!

The Payoff To Movement

Not only can you make exercise fun by using movement as the key, but this will also give you an incredible payoff by helping put you in the GFOM! When you exercise a cascade of chemicals is released within your brain, which causes a number of very positive changes. For our purposes I will only be reporting on a few of them. One in particular stands out which seems to show itself repeatedly in some very interesting places. Earlier in the book I described how researchers found that a certain neurotransmitter called serotonin (among others) was increased when you have had enough sleep. Well, serotonin is back again as a beneficial by-product when you incorporate plenty of movement in your life. Serotonin is important because it influences a myriad of things, including appetite control, sleep, memory, body temperature, muscle contraction, and, most importantly, mood! Serotonin, in other words, is one of those neurotransmitters that help put you in the

GFOM. Just like getting the proper amount of sleep has many benefits, so does regular exercise. **One reason you may not crave sweets as much when beginning regular exercise is that serotonin may also cause appetite suppression!** That's just one more reason to include movement in your life.

A second feel-good chemical, which will increase with exercise, is something called an endorphin. Endorphins are released by the pituitary gland after approximately thirty minutes of aerobic movement. Endorphins also put you in the GFOM by blocking pain signals to the brain and binding to opioid receptors, which give those who exercise the now famous "runner's high." The good part is that you don't have to run even a step to achieve this state of mind. All you need is thirty minutes of continuous movement where the pace is somewhat demanding, but not by any means exhausting. This euphoric feeling is guaranteed to place you in the GFOM. In fact, the best way to describe a runner's high for those who have never experienced it would be very brief: clarity and peace. A runner's high could very well give you one of the best moods that you will ever be in! You no longer view the challenges that you face as insurmountable, everything is achievable, and it is just a matter of doing it! You can think more clearly, communicate those thoughts far better, and also get along better with those around you. You see things so clearly that your True Vision becomes crystal clear and seems very attainable. One could even call it "runner's clarity," which can last anywhere from a few minutes to several hours. Being in this state (among other things) encourages you to train on a regular basis as you will want to do something that is not only good for you, but also places you in the GFOM!

We finish up our trio of feel-good brain chemicals that are prompted by exercise with phenylethylamine, otherwise known as PEA. According to the British Journal of Sports Medicine, PEA may be linked to the therapeutic effects of physical exercise on depression. PEA may also be able to put you in the GFOM.

The human body goes through a vast amount of change when movement is introduced on a regular basis. I don't think there is anything that is as effective for your physical and mental health as exercise! It can help you lose weight, gain muscle, look better, feel better, raise your self-esteem, and combat a number of diseases. Best of all movement can put you in the GFOM! What are you waiting for? Start moving around right now. Don't wait, use the Urgency Factor to get moving! You will feel the benefits almost right away, and your life will continue to improve in virtually every conceivable way!

Four More Activities That Help Put You In The GFOM

1. **Meditation**—For those of you who imagine a robed monk on top of a hill meditating, you are in for a big surprise. The philosophy of Buddhism is well known for its meditative practices although you need not be affiliated with any particular religion or philosophy in order to enjoy meditation. For example, I am a Christian and I studied this form of meditation several years ago, and was impressed with the meditative self-discipline of my teacher, who was a Buddhist monk. It doesn't matter what religion you practice in order to benefit from meditation. Many successful people from diverse religious backgrounds, such as Jerry Seinfeld and Gwyneth Paltrow, three-time Academy Award Best Director nominee David Lynch, and many Olympic and professional athletes, meditate for more relaxation and better performance. Meditation has been found to reduce stress, anxiety, and fatigue, lower blood pressure, and help you focus better in your daily life.

   Meditation is essentially nothing more than sitting quietly while breathing deeply and clearing your mind of all extemporaneous thought. Some forms of meditation use a word that must be said with every exhalation. However, this is not necessary. I have found that the most difficult part of meditation is clearing your mind as you breathe deeply. That could be one reason why some forms of meditation use a focus word so that your mind is focused on the word, and not on what activities you may have planned for the remainder of your day. Effective meditation quiets the mind. When a thought does come to mind, as they so often do, simply dismiss the thought and then return to your breathing. It may be helpful here to use the theater of the mind and picture a peaceful scene such as a sunset, a picturesque country scene, or any other relaxing image that you find soothing. Meditation has been described as "listening to the silence between thoughts." No, it isn't easy, but we know that nothing worthwhile, which carries with it long-term benefits, is.

Begin your meditation by setting a timer for two to five minutes. Increase your time by a minute or two every other time that you meditate. Work up to fifteen minutes four to six days per week. Some people meditate for much longer, and more often. However, for our purposes, many benefits can be gained by simply working up to fifteen minutes on a regular basis. If you don't like the idea of meditation, at least try to use one of the primary parts of meditation to your advantage, which is deep breathing. Let me share with you a highly beneficial deep breathing technique I learned from a holistic doctor. Breathe in for a count of four, hold it for a count of four, and then breathe out for a final count of four. Do this five times, five times per day. This takes only about five minutes for all five sessions, one minute per session. Either meditation or deep breathing requires only a tiny commitment of your time but will most definitely help place you in the GFOM.

2. **Prayer & Religious Services**—I can hear some of you say, "Meditation is cool, sure I can try that. But, what's up with praying and going to formal religious services? That doesn't sound like fun." Keep in mind that this chapter is about getting in and staying in the GFOM. If we can do that we are going to be more productive, more creative, and more open to successful thoughts and ideas. Are you open to new ideas right now? In order to achieve your True Vision you need to do what works. If you are excluding things that can help you because of some outdated preconceived notion of what works, then it is time to open your mind and look at the facts!

A Pew research poll found that people who attend regular religious services are happier than those attending less often and that those who seldom or never attend are least likely to be happy. If you think about it, this makes sense. Attending religious services regularly helps put you in the GFOM. When you believe in a higher power you are more likely to be able to release your stress and place it upon that higher power. Just as when we journal we are able to articulate our innermost thoughts and concerns, we can do the very same thing when in prayer. And unlike journaling, when we pray, we also feel that God hears us and understands our needs and desires.

The pat answer is, "I can pray at home, I don't need to go to a formal religious service." True, you can pray at home, and I hope that you do. However, you can't have meaningful social interaction with other like-minded people at home at this level. You are there together worshipping the same God (commonality), and interacting with each other (socialization). Both of these, in addition to having a belief in a higher power, help put you in the GFOM. However, it doesn't stop there!

When we attend religious services, we are also in a good position to help others. As you will read in the next segment, helping others is one more way to put you in the GFOM. Those who feel that they are spiritual need to attend formal services, if not for themselves then for the benefit that they are able to bring to other people.

If you do not attend because you find it boring then I suggest that you find a house of worship that is more suited to your liking. It is up for debate whether a house of worship that appeals to your intellectual side is also able to bring out your spiritual side, but at least try it. In the meantime, try attending a service that you think might be boring, and spice it up a little just by your presence. And keep in mind whether you are jumping up and down having a good time or not, most studies indicate that long-term attendance at a house of worship will indeed put you in the GFOM!

3. **Volunteer Work**—Volunteering helps us in many ways. When you are volunteering, you are no longer overly concerned about your own problems. It is almost like taking a mini-vacation from your personal concerns. Your perspective will change and you will suddenly become more thankful for the life that you have. Remember that you cannot be in a state of depression and thankful at the same time. Depression is rooted in (among other things) self-focus. I have never talked to any depressed persons who were also not overly focused on themselves. All that seems to be important is *their* past, *their* future, *their* health issues, *their* financial woes, *their* job, them, them, them. And what has all of this self-focus done for them? Remember the chapter on Total Focus? What you focus on expands. That means that worrying about your problems (as opposed to figuring out how to solve them and then taking action to do so) can actually make them

seem greater than they really are. Many times the best way to avoid feeling sorry for yourself, which can expand your sad (depressive) state, is to spend time helping someone who has far more problems than you will ever have! If you have never tried this, you will be surprised how good you feel after a couple of hours spent helping someone who is more in need than you are.

Recent research shows that volunteers obtain incredible benefits, such as lower rates of depression, greater longevity, and a lower incidence of heart disease. That said, I am sure you do not need a study to prove that helping other people can help put you in the GFOM. All you have to do is step up and try it. You will discover that when you help someone else you are also helping yourself in a multitude of ways!

Regardless of how busy you think you are, you can always find even one hour a week to help someone at some level. Consider volunteering to serve meals at a food kitchen or volunteering for a worthy cause or organization. Research suggests that volunteering 100 hours a year, or about two hours a week, rewards that individual with significant health benefits beyond being just emotionally uplifting.

When we help those in need become aware that someone cares about them, it also puts them in the GFOM, and what better way to help yourself than to reach out and help another human being? **We gradually discover in life that making ourselves happy has less to do with how much time we spend thinking about ourselves, and more to do with how much time we spend thinking of others. It is a seeming paradox.** Yet, in another sense, we never achieve great wealth by clinging to what we've accumulated, but rather by letting go and investing in an idea, product, or service. So too it is with helping ourselves emotionally. We must invest our time, talents and energy by helping others, and by doing this we reap a reward of happiness for ourselves, that GFOM!

4. **Laughter**—This seems like an obvious one to me. Then again I have been accused on occasion of laughing and making jokes at inappropriate times. My feeling is just about any time is a good time to have a good laugh. Many times people are just too self-conscious to laugh out loud and actually enjoy the moment.

Maybe they think that the moment will return. It doesn't, and it isn't going to. There might be moments that are similar, but that one is gone forever.

I have told my employees that if they are not having fun at work, then they are probably not doing the best job they can. Customers get a good sense of what a company's philosophy is very quickly from an employee's disposition. By smiling and enjoying your job, a positive and confident impression is given. When we enjoy ourselves, even with a little chuckle now and then, we not only put ourselves in the GFOM, but those around us as well. If you are in business, sales, personnel, education, the medical profession, or any position where you touch people's lives on a regular basis, you should be trying to cultivate this GFOM by being quick with a sincere smile, and ready to laugh or tell a joke.

Laughing releases those feel-good chemicals, endorphins and serotonin. And we end our brief laughter even happier than when we started. I believe that one of the greatest gifts we can give our children is a good sense of humor. Sometimes we have little more to carry us through some very difficult times in our lives than laughter.

The Humor Foundation website (I didn't know there was a humor foundation, did you? I bet they have a lot of fun at their meetings) states that there is new research in Japan showing laughter to be an efficient, low-cost medical treatment which helps reduce national health costs. Geneticist Kazuo Murakami considers that laughter is a stimulant, which can trigger energy inside a person's DNA that can potentially help cure disease. His research is published in the January 2006 edition of *Psychotherapy and Psychosomatics*.

If you are going through some difficult times in achieving your True Vision, know that there is light at the end of the tunnel. My advice is to keep laughing until you get there!

Chapter Ten (Continued):
Nutrition For The Glad Frame Of Mind

When you consume the proper nutrition it can trigger some of the same natural chemicals that are also released when you get the proper sleep, exercise, participate in certain activities and spend time with the right people. There are many foods and supplements available which have been shown in studies to raise the level of "feel good" chemicals in the brain, which help place us in the GFOM. Naturally before taking any additional vitamins and nutrients consult with your physician. Being in the GFOM, as well as being in good general health, takes a team effort!

Fish and Fish Oil

Studies show that fish oil is helpful in preventing heart disease, cancer, arthritis, diabetes and many inflammatory diseases. For our purposes, there are also certain types of fish and fish oil that are able to help put you in the GFOM. Documenting this is a study of 432 participants published in June 2010 in the *Journal of Clinical Psychiatry*. The study indicated that fish oil improved symptoms in patients who were diagnosed with depression. In fact, the improvement was comparable to those patients who were on more conventional antidepressant medication!

The reason that fish oil appears to have such a positive effect on mood is because of an ingredient called omega-3 fatty acids. Omega-3s are essential for good health, but cannot be made within the body and so must be consumed. These essential fatty acids play a crucial role in brain function as they promote the feel-good chemical we spoke about earlier, serotonin. In addition to helping put you in the GFOM, fish oil may also reduce the risk of heart disease. In fact, the American Heart Association recommends eating fish high in omega-3s at least twice a week.

Have you been getting all of the omega-3 fatty acids that you need? If not you might be feeling certain symptoms, which could include poor memory, fatigue and mood swings that may even put you in the sad frame of mind.

Omega-3 Fatty Foods

Fish oil capsules can give you similar benefits as eating fish several times per week. The point is that we have long known about the correlation between fish consumption and depression. Study after study has shown that the countries that consumed the most fish had the lowest rates of depression! One team of researchers found, for instance, that depression was sixty times higher in New Zealand, where the average person eats only about forty pounds of seafood per year, than in Japan, where the average person eats almost one hundred fifty pounds of seafood per year.

Here is a short list of ten fish that are high in omega-3 fatty acids; you want to aim for a serving size of at least 3.5 ounces. (The general rule of thumb when purchasing fish is a half-pound per person):

Mackerel—Spiny Dogfish—Herring—Sardines—Pilchards—Tuna (bluefin) —Trout (lake) —Sturgeon (Atlantic) —Salmon—Anchovies.

Whether you consume the right kind of fish two to three times per week, or regularly take fish oil capsules each day, or a combination of both, is up to you. Whichever you choose the evidence is mounting that fish oil and certain types of fish are very good at helping put you in the GFOM!

Vitamin D3

It is a well-known fact that some people are in the sad frame of mind during the wintertime when there is less sun. Seasonal Affect Disorder, or SAD, is said to affect about 11 million Americans. We also know that the problem occurs because of the lack of sunshine coming into contact with your skin. **When sunshine makes contact with the cholesterol in your skin, it stimulates the production of vitamin D3.** Vitamin D3 has an important role to play in your brain as it, too, may stimulate "feel good" chemicals that can help put you in the GFOM.

If you feel that you may suffer from seasonal depression, consult your health care provider about adding vitamin D3 to your diet, and in what amount. Recommendations vary greatly regarding how much vitamin D3 to take in order to ward off disease and improve your mood.

It is difficult to get the necessary daily vitamin D3 intake from the foods we eat. The best way to get vitamin D3 is, surprisingly, from sun exposure. About fifteen to twenty minutes of exposure of arms and legs at mid-day will provide your daily allowance of vitamin D3 naturally, which is always best. If you cannot spend time outside in a warm climate during the mid-day sun in your shorts and short sleeve shirt or swim suit, then you may not be getting enough vitamin D3, and supplementation should be considered. I have personally taken between 3000 and 5000 IU of vitamin D3 daily for several years and have felt a positive difference not only in my GFOM, but also in my workouts and general health as well.

The following are additional foods and nutrients that may put you in the GFOM. Always speak to your health care practitioner prior to changing your nutritional program.

Vitamin C

Vitamin C gained its reputation from many claims that it could prevent and shorten the common cold. Though the evidence is purely anecdotal I believe it to be true and have been a loyal fan of this supplement for several years. However, recent research has determined that vitamin C may also be quite good at helping put you in the GFOM by lowering the stress hormone cortisol.

A recent study subjected 120 people to a stressful combination of public speaking combined with math problems (I wonder where they got those courageous volunteers?). Half of the subjects were given two 500-mg sustained-release vitamin C capsules four times a day for two weeks, the other half a placebo. Stress signs such as elevated levels of cortisol were significantly higher in those who did not get the vitamin C supplement.

Lowering stress levels in your life will certainly help put you in the GFOM. You can do this through exercise, good nutrition, proper sleep and other lifestyle changes. Vitamin C supplements are perhaps another way (again, speak with your doctor first). In addition to supplementation I consume vitamin C-rich foods. A very short list of the many vitamin C rich foods include oranges, strawberries, black currants, kiwifruit, lemons, grapefruit and dark green vegetables such as kale, bell peppers and broccoli.

B Vitamins

A March 2005 article in the magazine *Alternative Medicine* stated that B vitamins are the most important vitamin supplement for improving mood! I never miss taking my multi-vitamin, which is loaded with all eight B vitamins. I also take extra folic acid and B12. It has been reported that B vitamins function as co-factors in the production of the neurotransmitter serotonin (hey, there's that word again). I will briefly focus below on two of the most important B vitamins that will help put you in the GFOM. Many authorities on the topic suggest that all B vitamins should be taken together as they work in synergy. The

B vitamins can be found in a high quality multi-vitamin and in many nutritious foods.

Vitamin B12

B12, found in meat, dairy products and eggs, helps to regenerate folic acid. In addition, B12 is known as "the energy vitamin." Certainly having more energy helps put you in the GFOM. Even more important, B12 is a precursor to the production of serotonin, the neurotransmitter we've been discussing that can positively affect your mood! But as B12 is not found in vegetables or fruit, vegetarians and vegans should consider taking a B12 supplement. A good quality multi-vitamin will have around 50mcg or more of B12. Since B12 can be taken in fairly high doses without experiencing any toxicity, many people decide to supplement this vitamin to an even greater degree. Some doctors who find their patients low on this crucial vitamin will even give vitamin B12 shots.

Folic Acid

Some studies have shown that people with lower levels of folic acid have a higher rate of depression. Most health organizations suggest an intake of 400mcg per day. This can be achieved by eating green leafy vegetables. In fact, the more vegetables you consume the more folic acid you will get. Do you eat 3 cups of vegetables and 2 cups of fruit per day? This is what the Centers for Disease Control recommends. **My experience has shown that loading up your diet with fruits and vegetables also puts you in the GFOM, and that vitamins work synergistically with other vitamins, causing each to be more readily absorbed by the body.**

According to an article in Reuters entitled "Healthy diet may benefit women's mental health," Dr. Felice N. Jacka, from the University of Melbourne, Australia, had this to say: "There's no magic diet. But eating a diet mainly of vegetables, fruit, whole grain foods, low fat dairy products, and lean meat, and reserving processed and sweet treats to 'sometimes foods,' will aid physical health and may also support mental well-being."

Foods rich in folic acid include the following: green leafy vegetables, spinach, oranges, nuts, seeds, beans, eggs, asparagus, and fortified breakfast cereals. If you think about it, a diet rich in fruit and vegetables makes sense for many reasons. Have you ever heard your doctor tell you to cut back on your vegetable consumption?

Chocolate (Cacao Beans)

Hey now we're talking! Let's all go out and have a chocolate bar and feel that GFOM! Well, not quite. Sorry to disappoint you, but the typical (milk) chocolate bar is loaded with so much sugar, artificial trans fats, and other undesirable substances that I recommend you stay away from it. Rather, consider getting your chocolate fix from almost pure dark chocolate like 70-year-old champion bicyclist Sandy Scott does (who is mentioned previously in the book). (Thousands of years ago the Mayans and Aztecs consumed a type of hot chocolate made from pure cacao beans.)

Dark unsweetened chocolate contains nutrients such as calcium, iron, phosphorus, potassium, and vitamins A, B1, 2, 3, 5, C, D, and E. Also, cocoa is one of the highest natural sources of magnesium. In addition to this, dark unsweetened chocolate (and the cacao bean) also contains an important flavonoid called epicatechin. Harvard Medical School Professor Norman Hollenberg has spent years studying the benefits of cacao drinking on the Kuna people in Panama. He found that the risk of stroke, heart failure, cancer and diabetes is reduced to less than 10% in the Kuna. Cacao beans in fact contain more antioxidants than virtually any other known food! I think that this is all quite amazing, how about you?

While dark unsweetened chocolate is important relative to health, the good news doesn't end there. It includes ingredients that can raise the levels of theobromine, phenylethylamine, and serotonin. All of them (especially our favorite neurotransmitter serotonin) are able to put you in the GFOM! It takes little more than one ounce of dark unsweetened chocolate per day to derive some positive effects. Try to find a chocolate bar that is at least 80% cacao, otherwise you are not getting enough cacao and worse, you will be consuming sugar and various artificial substances that won't benefit you in the end. You can also purchase cacao bean nibs (cacao beans broken into smaller chips) that can be eaten right out of the bag (caution: they are tasty but are not sweet). I like to sprinkle them on cereal, or toss them into the blender as an extra ingredient in my favorite health shake. You can even eat them by the handful right from the bag. But I caution you, cacao bean nibs are an acquired taste as they are not sweet.

Yogurt And Kefir

I really like both of these cultured milk products. Each is loaded with good bacteria (probiotics), which when consumed not only help to keep you healthy but also help to put you in the GFOM. Both fermented products are super foods for health, helping to promote a healthy digestive tract and a strong immune system. They are loaded with vitamins such as K, calcium (for strong bones), and iodine (thyroid function). They also have vitamin B2, vitamin B12 (for energy) and protein (for muscle growth). A 2007 study published in the *Journal of Medicinal Foods* showed that kefir has ingredients that may help target and stop the growth of human breast cancer cells. And both kefir and yogurt contain an amino acid called tryptophan, which can help elevate our serotonin levels and place you where? You guessed it, in the GFOM!

Recently studies suggest there could be a connection between the immune system and the central nervous system. That could be one reason that we might feel "butterflies" in the stomach when we are nervous or experience stomach ailments when we feel anxious or depressed.

Cultured milk products activate serotonin, but what really makes these foods superstars are the probiotics or good bacteria. These live microorganisms, studies show, can significantly decrease anxiety and stress in addition to improving general nutrition. Researchers studying the effects of probiotics on the emotional symptoms of patients with chronic fatigue syndrome found that "gut pathogens" are apparently able to communicate with the central nervous system and positively influence emotions.

In other words, both kefir and yogurt may have the capacity to put you in the GFOM! While more research is needed to reach a definitive conclusion, why wait to begin consuming kefir and yogurt today? See if it can boost your overall general health and help put you in the GFOM!

Sugar High

Did you know that you really do want to be in the GFOM? In fact, you want so much to be in this positive state that when you are not doing the many things suggested above your body is still trying to activate those feel good chemicals. That's why we experience cravings for sweets like doughnuts, cookies, candy bars and soda. Our bodies are telling us to raise the level of "feel-good" chemicals. Sugar and other carbohydrates have small molecular chains and are called simple carbohydrates. They activate many of the same feel-good chemicals as healthy foods, nutrients, exercise and other positive activities that we've covered. However, unlike those healthy foods and beneficial activities, a "sugar high" does not end well.

When we consume simple carbohydrates like those found in soda, for example, we get a quick surge of energy. The bad part is the letdown that occurs within an hour after, in addition of course to the empty calories we've just consumed. Unfortunately, the physical lethargy and sometimes sad emotional state of mind that can accompany this low cause the individual to return to the same poor food choices in order to achieve another temporary energy boost, or sugar high. This mood merry-go-round is made worse by the weight gain caused by the simple sugars found in soda and other junk foods, which are almost immediately stored as energy in the form of fat.

In addition, when we consume large quantities of these simple carbohydrates over time, the brain's endorphin sites start to slow production or even close to regulate the amount of endorphins in the brain. When this happens, depression of varying intensity follows. In other words, the thing that we are trying to increase, those feel-good chemicals, are eventually slowed when we consume too many simple sugars that are found in soda, candy, doughnuts, cookies, cakes and white-flour foods such as bread and pasta. Certain cereals which contain too much sugar are also able to move you toward the sad frame of mind. Not a very good way to start your day.

One athlete whom I trained once told me, "When I'm training I don't even crave junk food." That did not surprise me because when you are undergoing physical training, your body naturally produces those feel-good chemicals, so your craving for such foods either disappears or is greatly diminished.

Your body and mind want to feel good, and they will attempt to feel good any way they can. It is up to you to steer them toward the healthiest choices in order to ignite those feel-good chemicals and put yourself in the GFOM. **If we do not consciously seek out the positive nutrition and activities that we need, we will unconsciously** seek out those foods that temporarily activate the feel-good chemicals, ultimately leaving us in worse condition, both physically and emotionally.

Antidepressant Medication

According to the latest available statistics about 10% of America's population is on antidepressants. According to the CDC "Antidepressants were the most commonly prescribed medication during US hospital and doctor visits." One class of antidepressants is called selective serotonin reuptake inhibitors, commonly referred to as SSRIs. Sometimes slight abnormalities in brain chemistry will affect mood and behavior. According to leading medical authorities, SSRIs relieve symptoms of depression by keeping more serotonin in the brain as increased serotonin assists neurotransmission and improves your mood.

Antidepressants such as Celexa, Lexapro, Zoloft, Prozac, Paxil and others (SSRIs) work by keeping more serotonin in the brain, which improves mood. These medications must be prescribed and monitored by a physician. And similarly, you must not stop taking them without first getting approval from your doctor! However, consult with him to see whether engaging in these numerous activities, and consuming the many foods and nutrients that also produce serotonin in the brain, can help reduce or eliminate your need to continue taking SSRIs. While antidepressant drugs can have benefits they are not without certain side effects. Discuss the pros and cons with your health professional.

Base Building

As the various methodologies we've been discussing show, you have the power to put yourself in the GFOM, a place where you will be more productive, creative, and generally more successful. When you are doing the various things that move you in this direction you are building a base of strength. Having a strong base will help you deal with circumstances and challenges that may occur in your life, which sometimes may be out of your control. That strong base will prepare you emotionally for continuing on your path to success regardless of what might come your way. Being in the GFOM rather than in a negative state is what you need to take your True Vision all the way!

Certainly there are times when it is appropriate to be in the sad frame of mind. We all experience sadness when a close friend or relative passes on; we are angry when we feel we have been treated unfairly. And some may feel nervous or scared when walking down a dimly lighted street at night. These are all perfectly normal and healthy emotional reactions. However, with some base building there is no reason why most of your time cannot be spent in the GFOM!

Too often, though, I think people spend an inordinate amount of time in these negative states for no other reason than they just do not know how to turn it around! Could this be you? If so, why not give some, or even all, of the strategies on the previous pages a try? Before I try anything new I first ask myself, could this harm me in any way? If the answer is no, and there is a compelling argument for moving forward, I will usually give it a try. Why don't you look at improving your state of mind in the same way? For example, would getting seven to eight hours of deep sleep per night be a bad idea? Could consuming fresh healthy foods on a regular basis possibly harm you? Would avoiding the over-consumption of simple sugars (candy, soda, doughnuts, cookies and the like), which has been repeatedly demonstrated to harm your overall health and possibly leave you in a negative state of mind, harm you in any way? How about adding more movement in your life? Can you honestly say that you get at least five half-hour sessions of exercise-like movement per week? What about laughing more, attending church, learning to meditate (or practice deep breathing), doing volunteer work, spending more time with the people you love by being more social, and avoiding those negative people who tear you down? How could any of this harm you?

On the contrary, we know that successful people from all types of backgrounds are doing these very things, some very basic things. But champions are built by mastering the basics. **It's what you consistently put into practice on a daily basis that will eventually determine whether you win or lose in life.** Instead of just wishing you were a success at something that you've longed for, isn't it time that you joined them? Begin now to create a True Vision for putting yourself in the Glad Frame of Mind. It is one of the best presents you can give yourself and those around you as well!

As we move into the final chapter of this book I am going to focus on the importance of moving forward toward your True Vision, regardless of any difficulties and current unwanted circumstances. No path is without bumps along the way, and that's why it is key that you recognize the importance of getting in the GFOM. When we are in this state we truly feel like we can do anything! We feel able to take on more work and feel better about ourselves, in short, more in command of our destiny. We need to be in this state in order to overcome any challenge that may come our way. Learning to Never Give Up is an acquired skill which is best learned when in the GFOM. As you move forward in the GFOM you will be more able to accept any temporary setbacks and leap over those short-term obstacles, continuing on until you achieve your True Vision!

chapter eleven

VISION STEP:
NEVER GIVE UP!

It ain't how hard you can hit,
it's how hard you can get hit
and keep moving forward.
　　—Rocky Balboa

Do You Have What It Takes To Keep Your Vision Alive?

Do you have what it takes to keep your Vision alive, or will you stop moving forward the first time that things get difficult? In the end the one ingredient that seems hardest for people to do is to never give up under any circumstances! **I have often said that whatever I may lack in skill, I can compensate for with my deep-rooted desire to not give up under any conditions for any reason!** How about you? When you want something do you go after it, or are you deterred at the first sign of trouble?

We've all heard the old adage, "Nothing in life that is worthwhile is easy." I can personally attest to this, and I'm sure you can too. What makes achieving so difficult to begin with? I think it has something to do with all of the unknowns that we must ultimately face, and the many times that we have to actually repeat things before we get them right. Success in any endeavor seems to me (in part) to be about repeating something until we get it right and that takes persistence!

As a boy I remember watching an ant colony get wiped out after a big rainstorm. As I watched I remember thinking about all of the hard work the ants had put into piling one piece of sand on top of another, just to have it all destroyed in a matter of seconds. But then the next day after the storm had passed something strange happened. I walked past that very same spot and saw an ant struggling with a tiny piece of dirt. He was carrying it over to place it on top of all the other contributions being made by the many other ants helping to rebuild their home. I was amazed! They were determined, and in fact the rebuilding was well underway. Then it hit me, didn't they know how easily it could all be destroyed again? Didn't they realize how small they were, and that they were at the mercy of the slightest weather change? Not to mention people stepping on their home without even knowing it. Yet, there they were, dutifully rebuilding piece by painstaking piece, and I took notice and was impressed.

The ant seemed to me the king of persistence, relentlessly continuing on regardless of what may have occurred. What we learn from the ant is that success is a process and sometimes that process doesn't always move forward in a linear fashion. **Success is not a straight upward unbending line which leads immediately and directly to your True Vision.** Sometimes you can be so very close to achieving what you want; you're just about to place that last finishing touch on your Vision when out of the blue, just like that rainstorm, something happens to cause everything to tumble down. After the calamity, there you sit, head in hand. You must decide. Do you get back up to rebuild and start again, or give up?

Too Sensitive To Succeed?

Being a rational adult you're aware that you could get close again, only to have everything fall apart once more. So why not stay down? Why not quit? We know that if we don't move forward, especially after suffering that feeling of a loss, we will never win. So get back up and rebuild, and keep moving forward relentlessly, like a train screaming down the tracks! You can do this. Don't let anything stand in your way, especially your sensitivity to losing. Yes, I know it hurts. I have the scars to prove it. When I first began I was overly sensitive to any little thing that did not go my way. My feelings dictated which direction that I would move in. If something happened which caused things to stall

I would allow inertia to set in. Then I realized that if I kept moving ahead regardless of my temporary emotions things would eventually correct themselves by my continual efforts. You can only ignore your temporary feelings if you are tough enough to stop fretting over temporary loss and follow your long-term plan! Don't be so sensitive that you listen to that voice that tells you "it's all over," that voice is lying! That voice might be anything from your inner child who is afraid to keep going, to your so-called good friend who is secretly rooting for you to quit. Certainly, there are no guarantees in life. The more you try the more you can lose, but the more you can win too! While you may feel like you're losing repeatedly, you might only have to win one time to be a success. And that one time could be the next time you try! Stop being sensitive to loss and learn to move forward regardless of what your short-term emotions are telling you. Think beyond the moment, project your success into the future. Have you ever thought about it that way?

Too Imperfect To Succeed?

Do you pick on yourself as needing to be perfect? If you had it all together you would have obtained your True Vision by now, right? Is that your thought process? The people whom you think are perfect are usually the ones who have far more problems than you or I do. **I'm proud of the fact that I'm not perfect and that I know it. It's a good thing because I married an imperfect woman, and we have two imperfect children, live in an imperfect home, and I operate an imperfect business staffed with imperfect employees who in turn wait on imperfect customers who live in an imperfect world. Accept the fact that you're not perfect, and those around you will never be perfect.** The good news is that you can succeed anyway! You can succeed, that is, if you stop trying to be perfect, and accept the fact that you're going to make mistakes. When you do, don't give up, accept it for what it is, a temporary setback. Learn to look at your losses as temporary, because that's just what they are when you continue on. Setbacks are a part of the process of winning, and a very important process at that!

When we attempt to capture our True Vision we start out with a plan of action. However careful and well considered, more times than not it will have some flaws in it (just like you and I do), something that you didn't expect, and could not possibly have known about. Some of these obstacles may momentarily stop you dead in your tracks. Don't worry, you won't be the first person who has faced a challenge. Sometimes you need to move in another direction to get to the same place, make sense? This is when you try again in a slightly different way, a better way. You reroute. In fact, I can't think of any success that I've ever had that went so smoothly from start to finish that I didn't need to make a change at some point, and many times I've had to start all over. If an imperfect guy like me can do it, so can you!

Stop second-guessing yourself, you're never going to be 100% every time you make an important decision. Take the facts that you have, give them some thought and then make a decision. If you are wrong, then you've learned something haven't you? The next time you'll do better. The good part is the more decisions that you make, the better you get at it. It's called experience! And even after years of experience you will still not achieve perfection, not in this lifetime anyway. So stop trying to be perfect and move forward! Think of it this way: if you do nothing because you are afraid to make a mistake, in a sense you've already failed. I don't know of one True Vision that was ever achieved without taking that first step.

Disaster Strikes Out Of The Blue

Early in the development of my first business we suffered a devastating fire in one of the stores. We lost nearly all of that store's products. It was devastating financially as well as emotionally. It felt like someone had kicked me in the stomach as hard as they could and knocked the wind out of me. I was already short on cash as my bank credit line was all but tapped out. Nonetheless, there we were in the early morning hours, my first employee, Tony DiPierro and I. We had rushed to the scene, and were carrying out smoky electronics and appliances into the street, trying to salvage what we could. We knew that we were never going to be able to sell that inventory. It was ruined, but we continued to carry it out anyway, piece by piece like little worker ants trying to survive.

The irony of this entire episode was that we had a surplus of eight hundred dollars the month before (which was a rarity in those days), and we were so excited that we could choose between buying a copy machine or a new carpet for that store. Being customer-oriented my wife, Peggy, opted for the carpet in order to improve the appearance of the store. Unfortunately, I had no idea that within a matter of a few weeks that same new carpet would be destroyed in the fire along with so many products. Being vastly underinsured was just one more mistake that I added onto the heap.

During times like these you have to rely on the strong True Vision you've built. If that's missing then giving up is always an option. I'm convinced that's why so many people give up when faced with such a calamity. I can hear them now. "Why did this happen to me? This just isn't fair." Isn't that what some people say before giving up? Sometimes they bring fate into it. "If I was meant to succeed this would not have happened." When you have a strong True Vision you know that in the never-ending movie that plays in the theater of your mind you will never give up. You will always move forward regardless of whatever tragic circumstance tries to rob you of your True Vision. You see yourself succeeding, and you continue to move forward step-by-step, sometimes in half-steps, sometimes in emotional pain. You know that this too will pass (is there an emotion that doesn't pass?) and you will eventually be living your True Vision. Giving up is not an option. It's never an option, no matter what! If setbacks occur they must be looked at for what they are, a temporary learning process on the way to success!

There's a long list of calamities that can happen in business. You can suffer fire, theft, financial losses, and many other, sometimes unintentional self-inflicted catastrophes. It doesn't matter what your True Vision might be, you're always susceptible to some sort of miscalculation. If your True Vision is weight loss, setbacks can come in the form of a holiday, where it's hard to resist overeating. Even one particular weekend or an evening out can have severe dietary consequences. Whatever your True Vision, expect to be challenged and expect to work through it. The primary difference between those who succeed and those who fail is the fact that the ones who succeed just keep moving forward no matter what. Those are the people who have a True Vision, and will not let it go!

Sometimes in order to achieve your True Vision you must start over from scratch. If that's the case, always take time to count your blessings, even in the face of disaster. In the case of that store fire, I still had a few other stores left, and I was happy about that. I used the hand that was dealt to me and advertised a true fire sale from our temporary location. Business may have been off for a short time, but within a few months we were back in our former location, and doing as well as we ever did. I kept thinking that while this was a setback, it was not the end. I projected three to six months into the future, and could see that things would be fine. Sometimes it takes longer than that to come back from a temporary setback, but you will *come back*! That is, if you have a True Vision.

I can't predict what your problem will be. You could be one of the rare success stories that never suffer a setback . . . but don't count on it. I'm not being negative, I'm being realistic. So should you. I don't want you to begin anything thinking that you're going to succeed without having to fight for it. What happens to those who begin a venture with unrealistic expectations? Usually, the first time something bad happens they're ready to abandon their Vision and once again resume their trek on the path of least resistance. Human beings naturally want to do what is easy; after all we're emotionally created to avoid pain and discomfort. Overall that's not a bad thing—in fact it's a survival instinct. It helps us run from imminent danger; it's what causes us to quickly pull our hand back after inadvertently placing it on a hot stovetop.

Unfortunately, this built-in defense mechanism can also hurt us when it becomes a detriment to our quest to fulfill our True Vision. **When things go temporarily wrong, our natural instinct might be to stop doing what we're doing, and to retreat to a safe, secure place. A place where there are no challenges, no danger, and unfortunately, no success!**

Never thinking that anything could ever happen to you before you accomplish your True Vision is an unrealistic way to begin. In fact, this is one way to ensure that you *will* be running back to that safe, secure place, whether it is running to a comfort food that you shouldn't be eating, or staying in a job that you know you don't want to do for the rest of your life. The way to begin is with positive expectations. Knowing that will make you that much stronger and smarter when you do finally arrive! It is in the journey that we become worthy of achieving our True Vision. The key is to keep moving forward, in spite of your mistakes and the imperfection that the world offers up in every direction, especially when you think you can't!

The Process Drives The Event

I want you to have respect for the process of achieving your True Vision. To give you an idea of how the process drives the event I will use a simple comparison. Think of the tip of an iceberg that shows above the water as the event, and the actual iceberg that supports that tip as the process. While everyone sees the tip of the iceberg, they have no idea how large a base supports the top part of that iceberg, or how deep it goes. That's the difference in size and scope between the event and the process. **The process includes depth of accumulation and hard work and sacrifice, which builds the base for the event to take place.** The event is the actual accomplishment of your True Vision, what everyone sees. Keep in mind: when there's no process, there is no event! Ultimately the process drives the event.

For example, the next time that you're sitting in front of your television set cheering on your favorite baseball team, know that each one of the players worked thousands of hours to be where he is. Each of them sacrificed mightily to reach the level of professional athlete. Countless hours were spent in front of a pitching machine during hitting practice, fielding ground balls, fly balls, base running, etc. At any point in time any one of them could have said to himself, "This just isn't worth it. I'll never make the major leagues. Who am I kidding?" But they didn't. They trudged through all kinds of injuries, financial hardships, family problems, and all sorts of distractions. They did this because they have a respect for the process, and understood that without that process they were never going to arrive at the event, achieving their True Vision. They knew that the process drives the event, and without that difficult process they wouldn't have had a chance to play major league baseball.

It's easy to sit there and get caught up in an exciting event, like a great catch or a grand slam, but how many times have you ever thought of the work that a player puts in to make it to that point in his career? Obviously, it's not just professional baseball players that I'm referring to. Every professional athlete has also paid his or her dues in time, effort, and even pain. Every talented actor, actress, dancer, or musician has also gone through a process similar to that of the professional athlete. Countless hours are spent practicing, auditioning, rehearsing and working their way up. The process is about having an intelligent plan, and moving forward with that plan regardless of the obstacles in the way. If you can do this, you can accomplish almost anything! And I assure you, that you *will* be able to do this if you have established a True Vision for whatever endeavor you've seen come alive before your mind's eye.

What Process Must You Endure?

Most people struggle against one thing or another before they succeed. Each person has a different process to endure. The road to achieving your True Vision is not always about conquering others so much as it is about conquering your personal challenges. Know that others who realized their True Vision before you had to overcome handicaps and hardships just as you do. It is moving forward, sometimes in the face of various challenges, that finally yields success.

The following are several examples of those who have overcome adversity to achieve their True Vision:

- Movie star Tom Cruise is dyslexic.
- Popular late night talk show host and comedian Jay Leno couldn't even qualify as a store clerk because he failed the employment test at Woolworth's.
- Pop singer Christina Aguilera was abused as a child.
- Walt Disney's first cartoon production company went bankrupt.
- Movie star Bruce Willis had a serious stuttering problem growing up.
- Michael Jordan was cut from his high school basketball team as a sophomore because his coach didn't think he had potential!
- A corporate buyout of Handy Dan Home Improvement Centers forced two executives to lose their jobs. But Bernard Marcus, Arthur Blank and Ronald Brill began a company called Home Depot. It is now the largest home improvement center in the country!
- UCLA law school dropout Carly Fiorina worked as a Hewlett-Packard shipping clerk. In 1999 she became the first female CEO of a blue-chip company, Hewlett-Packard.
- Paul Orfalea was a dyslexic who failed second grade and was even temporarily placed in a school for the mentally retarded. He grew up to create Kinko's, the most successful photocopy chain in the United States.
- Dr. Seuss's first book was rejected by twenty-seven publishing houses. Not giving up, he went on to author more than forty best-selling children's books including *The Cat in the Hat* and *How the Grinch Stole Christmas*.
- 16 publishing agents and a dozen publishers rejected John Grisham's first novel.

- Peter Benchley, who was fired as a speechwriter for Richard Nixon, went on to write the best-selling novel *Jaws*.
- Ulysses S. Grant failed as a farmer, a real estate agent, a U.S. Customs official, and a store clerk. He went on to command the Union armies during the Civil War and was elected the 18th President of the United States in 1868.
- Thomas Monaghan, who was orphaned as a child, went on to become the multimillionaire owner of America's largest pizza chain, Domino's, and later on became owner of the Detroit Tigers.
- Sylvester Stallone was thrown out of fourteen schools in eleven years. At fifteen, his classmates voted him the one "most likely to end up in the electric chair." After struggling to graduate from high school, Stallone attended the University of Miami for three years but dropped out to pursue an acting career. He had many physical drawbacks. A trademark sneer, double lazy eyes, and slurred speech, the result of paralysis in the left side of his face caused by complications at birth, were certainly not an asset at that time.

  Stallone was turned down for even bit parts for years. He finally managed to land a few contracts as an "extra." One night, Stallone attended the Ali-Wepner fight. From watching that fight he conceived the idea of a boxing film. In three short days Stallone wrote the screenplay for the movie that would change his life forever. *Rocky* was that film, and Stallone wrote the script with the intention of playing the lead role himself. The script was repeatedly rejected because no one could visualize Sly Stallone in the role of a lead actor, but he had a True Vision for playing the lead, and that's all that was important! He could have sold the script alone several times and pocketed a good deal of cash. But in his heart he knew that no one could play the role of Rocky as well as he could. Finally, the quality of the script and the potential for success convinced a studio to take a gamble. I have no doubt that if today you could ask Sylvester Stallone if it was all worth it, he would without question give you a resounding yes!

What movie is playing in the theater of your mind? Is it one of victory? Do you see yourself smashing through walls to accomplish your True Vision? Going forward each day regardless of your temporary circumstances? There really is no excuse for stopping is there? We know that when we stop, give up, and walk away, we will most certainly not succeed. We must keep moving forward regardless of the circumstances that life has thrown at us. Ordinary people can do extraordinary things when a True Vision is playing in the theater of their mind.

Success stories in every walk of life are filled with people who kept on moving forward regardless of the odds they faced. Some people such as this next individual we'll meet were born with challenges that would be difficult for anyone to overcome. This person was born with above average challenges, but nevertheless created a True Vision of success and worked toward that Vision.

Sheila Radziewicz's "My Disability Is Not My Identity"

Sheila Radziewicz (Ra-Jar-idge) is a 32-year-old Massachusetts woman who was born with thrombocytopenia-absent radius (Thrombo-site-o-penia absent radius), referred to as "TAR" syndrome. This means that she was born without kneecaps and arms, and with one hand attached at each shoulder, two dislocated hips, two holes in her heart and her feet were pointed inward. However, that didn't stop her, or even slow her down. Her motto is "The impossible only takes a little longer." After speaking with Sheila Radziewicz one afternoon, I have no doubt that she can achieve the impossible, and indeed already has! Sheila drives a car with the assistance of something called "foot steering." This is an 8" disc that sits to the left of the brake pedal. "I also have a control area that sits next to my right hand. All the controls that are normally placed on the dashboard are in this little box." Sheila earned her Masters Degree in Criminal Justice in 2004 after attending Northern Arizona University, and if that notable accomplishment was not enough, after just 6 1/2 years of training she has also earned her black belt in Tae-kwon-do! This is an impressive achievement for anyone!

Sheila Earns Her Black Belt

I asked Sheila how she discovered the martial arts. "I saw a flyer at a coffee shop advertising martial arts and I thought that would be really fun, so I decided to go check it out. I don't see myself as having limitations so it didn't cross my mind that I wouldn't be able to do it." Many in Sheila's position would not be looking for such physical challenges. They would most likely not allow themselves a True Vision of achieving a black belt in karate. But Sheila is different; she has a Positive Self-Perception and an attitude which keeps her moving forward regardless of the condition she was dealt at birth.

Sheila has continued to move forward in her life even though her circumstances are far less than perfect. How many times have you put something off that you know you should be doing because everything was not quite lined up perfectly? "I had some very tough times during [Tae-kwon-do] practice," she admitted. "Sometimes I was so exhausted that I just wanted to go home and sleep, but I always came back for more!"

Maybe it was the strength instilled in her by her parents, doctors, and physical therapists. Then again, maybe it was the True Vision that Sheila had for taking what was given her and making the very most of it. "I was involved in a variety of sports growing up. My parents were told by my doctors to keep me active. I've roller skated, ice skated, skied, rode horseback, played soccer and danced." Nothing would stop Sheila Radziewicz from having a normal childhood, not even the fact that she was born with multiple disabilities. "My doctors and physical therapists never told me that I couldn't do something, and I was always encouraged by my parents. They would always say go ahead and try it, they would never say no."

We know that no one succeeds to any great degree solely on their own. She credits much of her early success in overcoming her personal challenges to Shriners Hospital for Children, which is a non-profit hospital network that helps children with disabilities. "They are located all over the world. I was brought to the hospital (in Springfield, Massachusetts) when I was 18 months old, and treated by Dr. Kruger."

Sheila's Difficult Early Days

It was never easy, especially to begin with. Sheila admits to some very difficult days as a child. "I had my days where I was sad, it was really hard and I didn't know if I could do it. I had a lot of people who were mean to me growing up. I had a lot of people who made fun of me, and stared at me, because of the braces I had to wear, and said really cruel things. Growing up with a disability was a hard thing. But my Vision was to keep moving forward no matter what, and that's just what I did."

Sheila went on to explain that it wasn't just the kids who could be cruel, but also the adults. "They wouldn't necessarily say anything, but they would stare at me, and just the look on their faces was very painful [to me]." Sheila went on to tell me that when she had her first few jobs as a teenager, she would see that look on adults' faces which said "you can't do that." However, this did not discourage her; it spurred her on.

"I questioned why I had to go through this when I was a child. There was a lot of pain, both emotional and physical. I had to learn to walk three different times after surgeries. After one surgery I recall my mother took off my braces so that I could get in the tub. She had to take my hand to help me walk. It bothered me because I could walk better before the surgery. Now I needed my mother's hand to walk, and that really bothered me. I was only 5 years old." Sheila then recalled the time when she and her father were coming home and the walker was in the car but she didn't want to use it. Her father looked at her and said, "Well then walk without it, Sheila." "'But it's hard Dad,' I remember saying." He replied, "If you don't want to use the walker then you just have to do it." "As I moved to take my first step out of the car my legs were so shaky I couldn't believe it. I was scared that I was going to fall, but I took one step, and then another. I was very determined as my father stood by my side, and cheered me on."

Sheila continued to tell me of her childhood battles which were only overcome by her True Vision to Never Give Up! "When I was five years old I had to have surgery on both of my legs. When I woke up from the anesthesia and looked down, I totally freaked out because I was in a full body cast." Unfortunately, it seemed to get only worse from there, "When they took the cast off I remember looking down, and seeing metal pins on each side of my thighs, imbedded in my skin. The next thing I remember is the most excruciating pain I have ever felt when they removed the pins. I remember screaming, and I was so loud that my mother heard me down the hall and around the corner. I was crying, it was so horrible and painful. They gave me pain medication, but it didn't always work the way they thought it would."

Sheila's life, while successful, has been difficult, but because of that difficulty she sees herself as a stronger person. "I'm proud of how things turned out. I don't ask why anymore. Life has been hard, but I wouldn't change anything. I understand that my disability made me who I am." Sheila recalls what her father would ask her periodically when she was feeling down and defeated, "Sheila what are you?" She would say, "I'm an American." Her father would then say, "What are the last four letters of American?" Sheila would respond, "I CAN." "Exactly," her father would say, "Exactly Sheila!" Sheila remembered, "And that would be the end of the discussion."

Today Sheila currently works a very demanding job as an advocate for victims of domestic violence; the end result of her True Vision for success was to be an accomplished, productive member of society, and she is certainly that—and more. At any point she could have tossed in the towel and easily given up, and who would have blamed her? However, instead she is helping others, not just through her chosen career path, but through her truly inspirational story. Instead of being the one who receives help, Sheila is the one who helps others! She told me that as a child, "I made up my mind I was going to make it, and that was it, and I never gave up!" She never gave up, but continued to move forward regardless of the difficulties that she had to overcome. "People sell themselves short, they are capable of doing far, far more than they think they can." Well said, Sheila, very well said!

What sort of challenges are you facing today? Are they as difficult as the ones that faced Sheila Radziewicz? As I have stated previously, everyone fights against or for something in their life. What is your controlling desire? Are you ready to do what Sheila did? Keep moving forward, never giving up?

Do you have what it takes to create a True Vision for your life and utilize all of the Vision Steps and not give up until you've achieved that True Vision?

Who Is Gene Mills?

I had the honor of interviewing Gene Mills for this book. You may be wondering, who is Gene Mills, and why would you interview him? He's not a familiar name, and unless you have followed amateur wrestling you probably wouldn't know him. He is considered one of the greatest amateur wrestlers America has ever turned out! With 1,356 career wins and 886 of those wins coming by pin, Gene Mills was to amateur wrestling what Muhammad Ali was to boxing, Michael Jordan was to basketball, and Wayne Gretzky was to hockey, all legends! If amateur wrestling were as popular in this country as any of these other sports, Gene Mills would be well-known to you whether or not you were an amateur wrestling fan.

Before some of you non-sports fans roll your eyes and skip to the next part of the book, I implore you to be patient and read on. It doesn't matter if you have never even played a sport outside of gym class. You can still learn much from Gene Mills and his True Vision. His story epitomizes what it is to have a True Vision, and to go forward hitting every single Vision Step on the way to incredible success! Discover how Gene Mills accomplished his True Vision for success, and model his dedication every step of the way so that you too can accomplish whatever True Vision that is playing in the theater of your mind.

The Gene Mills Story

Gene ran home after only two weeks on his high school's wrestling team, and announced proudly to his family that he loved wrestling and that he was going to be "good." His father Eugene looked at the ninth grader and asked, "How good?" Gene said, "Real good." Then his father said, "How good is real good?" Gene, undeterred by the line of questioning, responded, "I'm going to be great!" His father continued grilling, "How great Gene?" "I'm going to be the best wrestler ever!" Gene replied, with all the exuberance of a 14-year-old. Gene recalled that his father looked at him straight in the eye and replied, "Gene, no matter how good you ever get there will always be somebody better." Gene recalled, "That comment really ticked me off. I could see myself becoming a great champion, but apparently neither my father, nor anyone else for that matter, could see this Vision of mine."

Gene went on to tell me that very soon he was beating every freshman on the team right up to the heavyweight. He even defeated a returning varsity senior! No small feat for a guy 4'10" who was still only 88 pounds. Since he never had any formal training until that point, I asked Gene how this was possible. His reply was quite telling: "I had some natural abilities, and I used to wrestle around with my father who used to wrestle in high school. But I think the real reason was I never gave up! If someone got the better of me in one particular practice I would go home and think about how that happened and visualize what move I was going to use next time to counter it. I used to lose matches early on, but I never lost the lesson that losing taught me. I'd always visualize myself coming back and winning."

Mills was also a highly Effective Communicator, and thinking about the long-term gain, always asked for help from the best wrestlers in his area. "I was persistent. If I saw someone that I could learn from I would call him, or walk up to him at a tournament, and tell that wrestler how good he was, and that I'd like to get together with him so that I could get better." Gene used Effective Communication to his advantage, making sure that he approached the right person, at the right time, in the proper way.

Although small and somewhat scrawny for his weight, Gene never let that deter him. He would keep moving forward regardless of the circumstances, using every Vision Step available to him, including Positive Self-Discipline and the Urgency Factor: "I'd get up at 5:30 every morning and go on auto pilot. I'd put on my workout clothes and running shoes and go for a run before I was fully awake, and asked myself the stupid question, 'Do I want to get up and run?' If I asked myself that question before I got out of bed the answer would be 'no.' But I would get up and run anyway before I was wide awake enough to ask myself that question." Have you ever begun a workout program, and then talked yourself out of it before you even gave it a chance? Creating Positive Habits became second nature to Gene Mills as he tore through virtually every opponent he ever encountered in high school, college, and on the international circuit, beating the best of the best at every level!

Gene Mills Visualized Success

Visualization played a big part in all of that success. "I never ran to run. Yes, I ran to build-up my endurance, but what I liked about my running time was the solitude that it gave me. It was my time to visualize exactly what I was going to do to my opponents. **I visualized every move that I was going to throw, and how I would win. I visualized making my opponents so uncomfortable during our match that they didn't want to be out there with me anymore, and would quit.** If you've ever lost any sort of sporting event by one or two points, you always want to play them again because you think you can win. But, when you get crushed, I mean really destroyed, you want no part of that other team, it leaves a mark on you forever. That's what I wanted to do to my opponents. I had real Vision and was committed!"

Gene continued telling me about how he would pump up his True Vision with songs like "You're So Vain" (Carly Simon), "Taking Care of Business" (Bachman Turner Overdrive), and others as well. "As the years went on I would always find another song that could be applied to help with my Vision. I'd listen to my music and then in high school, for example, I could visualize myself pinning my way through to the state championship. When I was in college and wrestled internationally, I visualized the same thing to different music. While I didn't pin everyone, I worked harder than any other human being on the planet to be the best," says Mills, who incredibly never lost a collegiate regular-season dual match!

Mills continued to visualize himself as a champion, and regarded his opponents with pity. "I'd look across the mat before the match, see my opponent, and think to myself, you poor guy you don't know what you're in for tonight." Mills would make a quick evaluation of his opponent's physical attributes and think about how he would use those attributes against him. If his opponent had long legs, he imagined how much easier it would be to take the other wrestler to the mat with a double leg takedown. If the other wrestler was short, Mills would focus on using his leverage against the shorter man. If a man looked powerfully built, he would see himself being able to flip him to his back with a half nelson because the more muscular man might not have the flexibility to withstand that particular move. Mills emphasized, "There was always a reason why I should win." His Positive Perception quickly became reality!

Gene Mills is today a successful wrestling coach and even now uses visualization techniques on his team to boost their Positive Perception and build their True Vision. "The strongest part of the human body is the mind; I like to have my wrestlers visualize themselves out on the mat going through each move. In just ten minutes I can bring a wrestler through a visualization routine that will help him far more than running sprints, for example." Mills has his wrestlers visualize each move in detail and thinks quite correctly, that you must first see it in the theater of the mind before you can actually perform it in reality. This must sound familiar by now.

Olympic Gold Stolen, Not Lost

Even though Gene Mills earned the top spot on the United States Olympic team, the Olympic gold medal was stolen from him, stolen not by anyone on the wrestling mat, but by the political climate of the time when the United States boycotted the Moscow Olympics. This decision devastated every athlete on the United States Olympic team. Yet Mills nonetheless has the satisfaction of knowing that he decisively beat each of the three eventual medal winners in his weight class. In fact, he actually pinned the 1980 Olympic champion runner-up, 3rd and 4th place winners once just before the Olympics, and then beat the Olympic champion again two more times after the Olympics. As Mills put it, "I wanted him to make sure that he knew I was the best in the world." Missing the Olympics did not break Gene Mills. Others may have soured on amateur sports, or wrestling itself, and walked away. Gene Mills moved forward to a successful coaching career with the same Vision and personal drive that he brought to his wrestling days. As a coach he uses the same methodologies on his athletes that once inspired and guided his own wrestling career. As Mills summarizes it, "In my opinion 'Can't' is the worst swear word in the English language. I don't use it, and I don't allow any of my wrestlers to use it. You can never give up; you have to keep moving forward!" How very, very true!

Gene Mills epitomizes the very essence of True Vision. He carried the Vision crystallized in the theater of his mind out into the world, using each Vision Step along the way. He never gave up as he continued to move forward, and reached the very top in what is arguably the most difficult sport on the planet!

We all must overcome challenges to realize our True Vision. Some challenges appear like walls of ice, which at first seem impossible to climb, until you get a foothold and actually begin the ascent. You then develop a momentum all your own, which can only be defined as some mysterious force pulling you forward, sometimes inch by inch and then suddenly by huge strides. Once you build momentum you know that you cannot lose! You are in the process of achieving your True Vision. What possible reason could you have for giving up before you've felt the exhilaration of achieving that incredible feeling of accomplishment? Don't let the day-to-day grind halt you in your tracks. You can overcome whatever it is that has prevented you so far from living your True Vision. Realize that nothing worthwhile in life is easy, and that you may have to keep moving forward regardless of less than perfect circumstances. When things seem to go wrong and you suffer a temporary setback (remember they're all temporary when you have a True Vision) keep the following points in mind just before you're ready to quit . . . and then keep going!

What To Do When Things Seem To Go Wrong

1. **Immediately count your blessings.**
   By this I mean thank God for what you still have in your life that continues to go right. You'll immediately find a focus shift taking place. You'll stop worrying about what's wrong, and focus on what's right. This will give you an emotional boost, and help clear your head of all the negative thoughts that will inevitably dismantle your Vision piece by piece if you let them. **When we change our focus we change our minds.** When we focus on the negative that's what we become. When we focus on what's positive in our lives, even when things seem to be going wrong, we tend to gravitate toward being positive and to see the possibilities. Create a focus shift in your life when things are not going the way you'd like by immediately counting your blessings.

2. **Take a little time to project into the future.**
   How does this unexpected twist really influence your ability to succeed with your Vision? You'll usually find that if you project even one month into the future the problem you are worrying about will have little or no effect. When something goes wrong it's easy to overreact. Your mind races and fills with negativity, "That's it. I'm finished, I'll never make it now." Usually, whatever it is that went wrong might be far more insignificant than your initial reaction has determined. Ask yourself, how long will the issue actually take to overcome or resolve? Many times the problem is not as devastating as you think. Think again, and project a Positive Accurate Perception into the future.

3. **Record exactly what has taken place in your journal, and precisely what you plan to do about it.**
   Make sure you detail everything from how you felt when you first heard the upsetting news to the detailed steps that you will be taking to remedy the situation. Always end with a few positive affirmations. When my store suffered the fire, here is some of what I wrote in my journal the next day:
   "Early this morning one of my stores had a horrible fire, I was there early in the morning removing appliances and TVs. It felt like it was about 10 degrees outside. The whole thing seemed surrealistic to me. Where am I going to service my customers? I

will find a place tomorrow. This hurts but I know it's one more test that I'll pass with flying colors. One more time that I'll pick myself up off the ground and fight on. Sometimes things just happen. . . ."

When you write something down you seem better able to get your arms around the problem. You put it into its proper perspective. You also get to affirm, in writing, that you are going to succeed regardless of what may have happened.

4. **Ask For Help**
During trying times it's always good to be able to get help of any kind. Even if all you can find is emotional support, take it; sometimes, that's exactly what you need. Telling someone what happened and how you're going to come back from it is extremely helpful (like entries in your journal), and it also helps to clarify your own thoughts. No one succeeds in any great endeavor by himself; and you will not be the first I assure you! Depending on what your temporary loss may entail you may be in need of both emotional and financial help. One thing is for certain, you have a better chance of succeeding when you are not afraid to set your pride aside and reach out and ask (reread the chapter on communication if you have a difficult time understanding this). Remember that a setback is only temporary, that you must continue to progress toward your True Vision.

The only thing that you really have to do is move forward. You don't have to enjoy it; you don't have to feel that you're currently successful. There will be plenty of time for both of those to be felt at some point. Just hold on to your True Vision and know that others who have realized their own Vision have probably climbed higher walls than you'll have to, and succeeded. You're not alone! It's a tried and true path, and one that you can well achieve. As long as you have a True Vision you can, and will, keep moving forward!

5. **Understand Failure For What It Really Is**
What is failure anyway? Have you ever really thought about it? Here is my definition: Trying something and not succeeding as you had planned. That's it. It doesn't sound so scary when you think of it this way, does it? What may bother you most about failing are the negative emotions you attach to failure, which can

cause you to get into a sad frame of mind. Feeling like you've let others down might also be a part of it. And there is the public humiliation you may feel when you have failed. But most people are too concerned with their own lives to pay much attention to what you're doing. However, we live in an age where we get instant feedback, which can be both good and bad. Some may laugh at your temporary setback, some may be quick to criticize you. I've learned through the years that no matter what you do there will be critics. And usually these are the types of people with whom you just can't win. They'll point a finger if you fail. If you succeed, they will become jealous and try to denigrate your efforts in some way. "He was just lucky." "I heard that his father gave him most of the money to start that business." "Yeah, she lost weight, but I heard it was all because of liposuction." So what do you do?

The answer gradually became obvious to me over a period of years. Don't invest others with the power to control what you do or how you feel. Trust me, it took me a while to understand this, but once I did, I was free, free from that small group of people that will never know real success because they've never tried to accomplish anything of magnitude and never will. They're content to sit on the sidelines of life throwing rotten tomatoes at anyone who tries to make an improvement in their own lives. Don't hate these people, it should be obvious that they have enough problems of their own. Above all, don't let them dampen your desire to accomplish your True Vision by controlling how you think or feel about yourself, or tell you what your next move should be. Simply understand that people like this have always existed and will continue to exist as long as human beings inhabit this planet. Understand and move on.

Aside from the meaningless comments of the naysayers, sometimes we're not exactly sure what it is that we don't like about failure, but we know we don't like it. We all want to win every single time. But the irony of this is that you can't be afraid to fail in order to succeed. The only way you have the opportunity to succeed at anything is if you also have the opportunity to fail. Success and failure are really two different sides of the same coin flip. The good part is that in this game, how the coin toss lands is largely up to you! If you get it wrong, and it comes up tails instead of heads, as you wanted, you get to flip it over again. That is, if you are not afraid that it might come up tails.

Try to look at failure as getting the wrong side of that coin. Is that disgraceful? Not to me, and I hope not to you either. That's really all failure is. Most people are afraid that the right side of that coin will not come up, every time they flip it. Or, they are afraid perhaps that the right side will never come up. It bothers them because they associate the wrong side of the coin popping up with not being good enough as a person. Have you ever done that? The internal dialogue sounds something like this: "I failed, I'm no good. I can't get anything right." That is a harsh, sweeping, inaccurate conclusion—and it's wrong! A more accurate assessment would be to leave the emotion out, focus on the exact things that you learned from that temporary setback, and then work to not repeat them the next time. Separate the emotion from the facts. That's not hard to do with a little practice.

As you move forward (and you must keep moving forward) remember this: You are not your failure! You are separate from your failure. You only become a failure in your own mind when you cloud your assessment with thoughts that are emotional half-truths instead of with the facts, and then quit and walk away. You are a human being, created by God, trying to achieve something that is important to you, and you must have the courage to try again! Maybe you didn't get it exactly right the first time, not many people do. In fact, you may not get it right time after time, but so what? If each time you try, and each time you don't quite get it right, you have learned something of value, and you are actually better off than before you began. **While you may own your failure, you cannot let your failure own you!** Keep moving forward, and know that you are not your failure. Never let anyone, especially you, keep you from achieving your True Vision!

I have had the following poem hanging on my wall for over 25 years. I would love to give the author credit, but he or she is unknown. I have found that simple little poem has inspired me, especially during times when things seemed to be going in the wrong direction. Many times when I felt like quitting, this poem reminded me of my True Vision, and I kept moving forward. I would read the poem and imagine the many others who, like me, were ready to quit, but pushed on to achieve their True Vision. Sometimes all you have to do to win is to keep moving forward. That is the most difficult thing to do when every fiber in your being wants to quit.

Don't Quit

When things go wrong, as they sometimes will,
When the road you're trudging seems all uphill,
When the funds are low and the debts are high,
And you want to smile, but you have to sigh,
When care is pressing you down a bit,
Rest, if you must, but don't you quit.

Life is strange with its twists and turns,
As every one of us sometimes learns,
And many a failure turns about,
When he might have won had he stuck it out;
Don't give up though the pace seems slow—
You may succeed with another blow.

Often the goal is nearer than,
It seems to a faint and faltering man,
Often the struggler has given up,
When he might have captured the victor's cup,
And he learned too late when the night slipped down,
How close he was to the golden crown.

Success is failure turned inside out—
The silver tint of the clouds of doubt,
And you never can tell how close you are,
It may be near when it seems so far,
So stick to the fight when you're hardest hit—
It's when things seem worst that you must not quit.

Final View

> "A truly good book teaches me better than to read it.
> I must soon lay it down, and commence living on its hint.
> What I began by reading, I must finish by acting."
> —Henry David Thoreau

The nineteenth-century writer James Allen observed that "People are anxious to improve their circumstances, but are unwilling to improve themselves; they therefore remain bound." Unfortunately, this assessment does describe many people, but I doubt it describes you. You are different because you are either trying to develop a True Vision, or have one, and are looking for direction and the skills needed to succeed. It is my hope that this book will make a positive difference in your life. It is my hope that you understand that you *can* help yourself. You *can* change. You *can* get it done! You are on your way to building your own True Vision and you will not be stopped!

Think of this as a new beginning. Unlike any of the other times that you may have tried to make a positive change in your life, this time it's for real! You have in your hands right now enough information to get just about anything that you want. Make sure that you do not pass it by.

When it comes to the topic of success, a story probably told and retold through the years comes to mind.

The Touchstone

When the great library of Alexandria burned, the story goes, one book was saved. But it was not a valuable book; and so a poor man, who could read a little, bought it for a few coppers. The book wasn't very interesting, but between its pages there was something very interesting indeed. It was a thin strip of vellum on which was written the secret of the "Touchstone"! The touchstone was a small pebble that could turn any common metal into pure gold. The writing explained that it was lying among thousands and thousands of other pebbles that looked exactly like it. But the secret was this: The real stone would feel warm, while ordinary pebbles are cold. So the man sold his few belongings, bought some simple supplies, camped on the seashore, and began testing pebbles.

He knew that if he picked up ordinary pebbles and threw them down again because they were cold, he might pick up the same pebble hundreds of times. So, when he felt one that was cold, he threw it into the sea. He spent a whole day doing this but none of them was the touchstone. Yet he went on and on this way. Pick up a pebble. Cold— throw it into the sea. Pick up another. Throw it into the sea. The days stretched into weeks and the weeks into months. One day, however, about mid-afternoon, he picked up a pebble and it was warm. He threw it into the sea before he realized what he had done! He had formed such a strong habit of throwing each pebble into the sea that when the one he wanted came along, he still threw it away. So it is with opportunity. Unless we are vigilant, it's easy to fail to recognize an opportunity when it is in hand and it's just as easy to throw it away!

I understand only too well that you may have traveled down a similar path in the past looking for success and only coming up with a cold pebble in hand. I want you to separate those experiences from what you currently have in your hands. I want you to develop a True Vision for success in your life, whatever your challenge may be. I think that most people want to change at least one part of their lives, yet for one reason or another they have just not been able to do it.

There are many reasons people lose faith in their own ability to make positive changes in their life and to capture that True Vision. Sometimes they have failed at it, and those negative emotions tug at them, holding them back, and they cannot muster the will to move forward. Sometimes the task at hand appears too difficult, and they quit before they begin. Still other times, they think that something will happen out of the blue and they will suddenly be transformed into the person that they have always wanted to be. I never rule out miracles, as I have seen God work some very mighty miracles in my life and in other people's lives as well. However, I ask you to look at whatever ability God gave you as a miracle, and know that when you use that ability you are giving a gift back to God. Instead of giving your gift to God, are you going to sit there feeling helpless, look up at God, and complain that His gift was not quite good enough for you? Would you ask for a larger more expensive gift from a loved one who gave you exactly what you needed, and nothing more? Whatever your True Vision might be, is it so difficult to believe that you can succeed if you work to the best of your ability with what God already gave you, right here and right now?

That does not mean you shouldn't pray or ask others for assistance.

I hope that you do both of these things. But in the end the answer rarely lies in waiting for help to arrive. The answer lies within you! There is nothing more personal that can lie inside of someone than his or her own True Vision. I challenge you to start today and create a crystal clear positive movie in the theater of your mind of exactly what you want to do, based upon your own desires, talents, and what you are capable of learning. Why wait any longer?

I know that having a True Vision can change your life for the better! However, you have the final say on whether or not you will take the information in this book and act on it. It is time for you to exercise one more gift from God, *your free will*, and begin to move your life in the right direction. You can certainly choose to close this book, set it down, and walk away. Time will then eventually erode everything that you have read, everything that seemed to ring true, everything that you felt would work in your life if you had only acted on the knowledge. Unless you put into practice what you have learned it most certainly will leave you like a newfound friend who has been neglected. Don't allow that to happen. Decide right now to create your very own True Vision, following all of the Vision Steps carefully laid out in this book.

Whichever direction you choose to move, do just one thing for yourself, decide right now! Don't allow time or distraction to make the choice for you. Don't let one more day, hour, or minute pass without making that decision. If you choose to do nothing, tell yourself exactly that: "I am going to do nothing." How does that sound? If you choose to do something, but not right now, then in reality you are choosing to do nothing! What you are doing is hedging your decision not to move forward by making yourself feel better. I call that padding your failure. By softening the blow you become numb to your own loss, and there is less pain involved in failing. Ask yourself this question, when you did nothing in the past, did it ever help to initiate positive change?

If you decide to move ahead right now with your own True Vision, congratulations! You have just chosen a path that will reap many rewards for you in the future. It is a path that is filled with excitement and challenges, peaks and valleys that truly will be the most exciting ride of your life! It is a path that will lead to a destination that is many times better than where you began. But the key is to first begin, isn't it? There is never a happy ending without there first being a beginning. There is never a happy ending without there first being a smart workable plan that is put into action with devotion and tenacity. There is never a happy ending without first continuing on sometimes through difficulty. Finally, there is never a happy ending without there first being a True Vision playing in the theater of the mind of what you want that happy ending to look like!

As Henry David Thoreau wrote: "I would give all the wealth of the world, and all the deeds of all the heroes, for one True Vision." It is my sincerest wish that you create a True Vision, go forward with desire and act on it immediately!

The time for you to choose is now!

EPILOGUE

As I sat shuffling through my notes I still had a difficult time seeing all of it forming into a book. I needed to increase my True Vision. I drove to the nearest bookstore and stood in front of the section of books where True Vision would be sold. I visualized the book spine with the words *True Vision 4 Success* standing out among the others. It had a certain glow about it. I could see its color and shape clearly in the theater of my mind. I could then see and hear people walking up to that particular section of books and scanning with their eyes each title. I viewed them one by one settling on *True Vision 4 Success* as they picked it up and held it in their hands. As each thumbed through the book I could see them gain interest. I could clearly picture their focus intensify as each was reading something that would help them. They then walked over to the checkout line and made the purchase. I could see this happening in the theater of my mind as my True Vision grew for writing this book. The theater of the mind is indeed a very powerful place!

This book didn't just come together; nothing of value ever does without hard work and a good plan. However, now I had a True Vision for the end result. I clung to my True Vision through many long days and nights of working on this book. True Vision is certainly the one thing that keeps you fully directed with purpose working consistently through difficult times late into the night.

My True Vision for success was to publish this book. I hope that you enjoyed my True Vision and develop one of your own.

ACKNOWLEDGMENTS

As I have said many times in the past, no one succeeds in any worthwhile endeavor alone and I am certainly not the first. While I never expect any new project to be easy, I was actually surprised by the amount of work that has gone into this book. It was truly a challenge to put all of my notes together from so many years of involvement with so many different ventures, personally and professionally. I am very thankful first of all to God for giving me the good health and energy to continue on with this project while juggling so many other things.

If I were to go back and thank all of the people in my life who have taught me by example, whether meaning to or not, I could write an additional book for that alone. For now I want to thank not only those who have helped me through so many of my ventures, but those who have meant so much to me as well.

To my wife Peggy who has always been my most loyal and steadfast supporter, also my very first one! With her encouragement through the years I have truly felt that I could do anything. Not coincidentally she is also the very first person to read this book in manuscript form, cover to cover. To my children Marianne and Bobby, they have been my pride and joy through the years. There is nothing in this world that can take their place and I am exceedingly proud of them and have tried to instill in their maturing minds a True Vision 4 Success as they grew. In memory of my father Sam who just recently passed. More than anyone he taught me the value of hard work and self-discipline. Not by talking about it, but through his actions every day of his life. He would rise early to go to work and after arriving home he would continue working on his many projects. He seemed like perpetual motion to those of us who tried keeping up with him. As a child I could not have asked for a better example of what it takes to succeed. In memory of my mother Ella who dedicated her life to her husband and family and also taught me the importance of saving. Her ability to stretch a dollar and always have enough left over to make sure that I always had the essentials and even some extras was at once both an act of love and skillful money management. Her grace and compassion were unparalleled. I still feel her loss, and suspect I always will.

In memory of the toughest training partner that I ever had the opportunity to work out with, Scott Cannova. Scott helped me train to be recognized by GUINNESS WORLD RECORDS for a record in chin-ups. He was a state champion power lifter with a 677 pound deadlift and a bench press of over 400 pounds, all at a bodyweight of only 178! But he was far more than a training partner, he was also a good friend for many years and a kindhearted person who was always ready to help.

To Anthony DiPierro who has been by my side for every sizeable venture that I have ever launched. I cannot imagine having the success that I have had without Tony's insightful wisdom, compassion, his constant desire to give far more than he has to, and of course his many prayers. Proverbs 18:24 best describes our relationship: ..."But there is a friend that sticketh closer than a brother."

To Gary Mace, Mark Virkler and Jim Nabywienic who have in every way been builders of men. It is through their examples of hard work, honesty and especially loyalty that have encouraged me on to new and bigger ventures. Specifically, Gary with financial projections and budgeting, Mark's mental toughness and ability to get things done, and Jim's shear charm and great skill in communicating all that is positive.

To Dave McKeon a banker who had vision. Dave was responsible for giving my first large company a loan that it needed to expand. Because of Dave's vision for my company we were able to open an average of one store per week for two years! Without Dave's assistance it would have been much more difficult to grow the company to its full potential.

Finally, to Robin Hamm who proofread these pages, created the cover design, and helped with some of the research and the massive coordination effort.

To all of you go my many thanks!

Permissions

The longer quotations in this book came from the following sources:

Nicklaus, Jack and Ken Bowden. *Golf My Way.* New York: Simon and Schuster, 1974.

Borum, Randy. "Inside the Heart & Mind of a Champion." *TapouT Magazine.* 1997. Print.

Borum Randy. "Inside the Heart & Mind of a Champion." *Combat Sport Psychology.* Web. 20 Sept. 2010. <http://combatsportpsychology.blogspot .com/2008/01/inside-heart-mind-of-champion.html>.

Hill, N., *Think and Grow Rich; Teaching, for the First Time, the famous Andrew Carnegie Formula for Money-Making, Based upon the Thirteen Proven Steps to Riches.* The Ralston Society, 1937.

Gladwell, Malcolm. *Outliers: Why Some People Succeed and Some Don't.* Little: Little, 2008.